Company Tax Planning Handbook 2015/2016

Lee J Hadnum

IMPORTANT LEGAL NOTICES:

WealthProtectionReportTM
TAX GUIDE - "Company Tax Planning Handbook 2015/2016"

Published by:
WealthProtectionReport.co.uk
Email: sales@wealthprotectionreport.co.uk

Second Edition: September 2015

Copyright

Trademarks

DISCLAIMER

CONTENTS

2014

Summer Budget

Other WPR Tax Guides

ABOUT THE AUTHOR

Lee Hadnum LLB ACA CTA is a UK tax specialist. He is a Chartered Accountant and Chartered Tax Adviser and is the Editor of the popular tax planning website:

www.wealthprotectionreport.co.uk

You can join Lee's Tax Coaching Club at:

http://www.wealthprotectionreport.co.uk/products/item70.cfm

and can e-mail Lee directly at:

Lee@wealthprotectionreport.co.uk with tax planning questions

Members of www.wealthprotectionreport.co.uk can access thousands of articles and free tax planning books.

Lee is also the author of a number of best selling tax planning books including:

- **Tax Planning Techniques Of The Rich & Famous** - Essential reading for anyone who wants to use the same tax planning techniques as the most successful Entrepreneurs, large corporations and celebrities

- **The Worlds Best Tax Havens** – 220 page book looking at the worlds best offshore jurisdictions in detail

- **Inheritance Tax Planning Handbook** – Detailed tax planning for anyone looking to reduce inheritance tax.

- **Non Resident & Offshore Tax Planning** – Offshore tax planning for UK residents or anyone looking to purchase UK property or trade in the UK. A comprehensive guide.

- **Tax Planning With Offshore Companies & Trusts: The A-Z Guide** - Detailed analysis of when and how you can use offshore companies and trusts to reduce your UK taxes

- **Tax Planning For Company Owners** – How company owners

can reduce income tax, corporation tax and NICs

- **CGT Planning Handbook** – Tax planning for anyone looking to reduce UK capital gains tax

- **Buy To Let Tax Planning** – How property investors can reduce income tax, CGT and inheritance tax

- **Asset Protection Handbook** – Looks at strategies to ringfence your assets in today's increasing litigious climate

- **Working Overseas Guide** – Comprehensive analysis of how you can save tax when working overseas

- **Double Tax Treaty Planning** – How you can use double tax treaties to reduce UK taxes

1. INTRODUCTION

Using a UK company can be very attractive for a number of reasons. Crucially though:

☐ It is classed as a separate legal entity and can sue and be sued in its own name. It can therefore be useful for asset protection purposes and

☐ It is subject to much lower rates of tax than an individual.

The highest rate of personal income tax is currently 45%. However the highest headline rate of tax a company pays is 20% (from April 2015).

This can represent a significant benefit, particularly where business owners retain profits within the company.

The Government is keen to reduce the rates of corporation tax. They have reduced it from well over 30% to just 20% from April 2015. It is to be cut to 19% in 2017, followed by a cut to 18% in 2020.

Even though the tax rates are reducing, company owners will still be looking at opportunities to further reduce the company and personal taxes they will be liable to.

In this book we look at a variety of different aspects of tax planning for companies and company owners.

CHAPTER 2
WHY USE A COMPANY?

In this chapter we'll recap on the main reason for using a company.

The main benefit in using a company is that it is taxed separately from you as an individual.

Therefore if you traded in your own name you'd be taxed at 20%, 40% or 45% depending on the level of the profits/your income.

If you trade as a limited company the company will pay tax at the rates of 20%.

For anyone with income/profits above the higher rate tax band there can therefore be significant advantages to using a company.

The level of corporation tax will be significantly less than the level of income tax if they traded in their own name.

Of course this isn't the end of the matter. There is also income tax to take into account when the shareholders extract profits from the company. This is now usually structured as dividends as they now result in a larger take home pay then a salary payment.

The income tax charge on the extraction of funds from the company significantly reduces the tax attractiveness of using a company, particularly where all of the profits are extracted.

The tax rates on dividends (25% for higher rate taxpayers and 30.55% for additional rate taxpayers) as well as the corporation tax charges pretty much eliminate the tax benefit of the lower rates of corporation tax.

However, where profits are retained in the company – or at least some of the profits are retained in the company, there can still be significant advantages to using a company.

This is the main reason for using a company: The ability to reinvest profits allows for a deferral of the tax payable.

Of course if the profits are extracted in the future there would then be income tax payable, but you could look to extracting free of tax as a non resident or liquidating the company and extracting as a capital distribution (potentially paying just 10% CGT).

CHAPTER 3
SHOULD YOU EVEN BE USING A COMPANY?

Much has been written on when you should use a UK company. As we've seen above, the ability to reinvest profits can lead to a significant reduction in the total tax payable. However, this is not always the case. There are occasions when using a UK company can actually increase the amount of tax payable.

We've listed some of the main occasions below:

If you're planning on going overseas

This is something that many people overlook, but given the number of people emigrating and working from overseas (eg telecommuting) it's well worth bearing in mind.

Imagine this. You write a few e-books and decide to sell them over the internet. As you live in the UK you know all about the advantages of a UK company and therefore transfer the rights to the books to the company at start up and trade via the UK company.

Five years later, the company has become profitable, and generates royalties of £75,000 per annum. You have got sick of life in the UK and want to move to Cyprus.

There is no problem with you personally moving to Cyprus, the downside is that the e-books are locked in the UK company. Any transfer of the e-books out of the UK company would crystallise a gain in the UK company, based on the market value of the books (likely to be substantial if they're generating £75,000 pa) and the original acquisition cost (nominal).

Therefore the fact that you never set foot in the UK would not stop the UK taxman taking 20% of the profits of the UK royalty company.

The fact that Cyprus is generally regarded as a royalty tax haven wouldn't matter to you as you wouldn't be able to take advantage of it (at least not without incurring a hefty tax cost).

The other downside of retaining a UK company is that you can't completely sever your ties with the UK, as you'll still be in receipt of UK dividends. You could incorporate an overseas company to hold the shares but this involves more reporting and incorporation fees.

If you're trading personally you won't have any of these problems.

There is no deemed disposal of assets when you cease to be UK resident (unlike in many countries) and you could just carry out the trade from overseas. Provided you have no UK trade there will then be no UK tax charges.

Occupying property

If you're looking at purchasing property which you will or even may occupy this should not be owned by a company.

The use of a company in this case has a number of disadvantages including:

☐ The fact that the property will be locked in the company.

Any disposal of the property would crystallise a gain in the company (subject to corporation tax) as well as a further tax charge on the extraction of the proceeds

☐ The reliefs available to a company are much less than an individual. In particular if you have occupied the property as your main residence you would qualify for principal private residence ('PPR') relief on a disposal. In addition the annual exemption would be due. This will in many cases fully eliminate any gain.

By contrast a company would not be entitled to any of these reliefs and would be fully charged to corporation tax on the gain with only a small amount of relief for the effects of inflation.

☐ Any occupation of the property by you without you paying the company a market rental would be classed as a benefit in kind from the company to you. The broad effect of this is that you are likely to be subject to an annual income tax charge on approximately the market rental income the company could have obtained.

☐ The company would be subject to the Annual Tax on Enveloped Dwellings (ATED) provisions.

The ATED was introduced in April 2013, alongside higher rate SDLT and the ATED-related CGT charge, for residential properties owned by companies worth over £2 million.

There is an exemption for the ATED charge for properties let out on commercial terms.

It was announced in 2014 that the ATED will apply from 1 April 2015 to UK residential properties owned by a company worth over £1 million but less than £2 million, and from 1 April 2016 to such properties worth between £500,001 and £1 million.

The new ATED charge for interests between £1,000,001 and £2 million will be £7,000 for the chargeable period from 1 April 2015 to 31 March 2016.

For interests between £500,001 and £1 million the charge will be £3,500 for the chargeable period from 1 April 2016 to 31 March 2017.

Therefore owning a personal residence via a company, is in many cases a big no, no.

If you're a non UK domiciliary

If you're a non UK domiciliary you are generally taxed on overseas income and gains to the extent that the income or proceeds are remitted to the UK (ie brought into the UK) if you make the claim.

In this case, if you own overseas assets or are conducting a trade overseas using a UK company may not be advisable.

A UK company would usually be classed as resident in the UK, and as such would be subject to corporation tax on its worldwide income and gains.

Given as a non UK domiciliary you could own personally and avoid UK tax by retaining income or gains overseas using a UK company would not be advisable (providing you could retain some of the cash overseas).

Incorporation followed by a quick sale

Transferring your business to a company could be disastrous if you are then made an offer you can't refuse for the shares.

As the owner of the unincorporated business you could probably sell benefiting from Entrepreneurs relief (ie the 10% rate of CGT on gains of up to £10,000,000).

When you transfer the business to the company, you then own the shares and a new period of ownership begins. A disposal of the shares within twelve months of the share acquisition would not entitle you to any Entrepreneurs Relief.

Even if you incorporated the company years before and left it dormant you wouldn't have more than one year qualifying ownership as the company would only be a trading company when the trade was transferred into it.

Assets held long term

If you're holding property or assets long term for investment potential buy holding via a company, the company loses out on the 28% rate of capital gains tax.

The company would only get meagre indexation relief with any gains then subject to corporation tax at 20% and a further income tax charge (likely to be at 25% or 30.55%) on the extraction of profits.

You could always sell the shares in the company instead of the company selling the assets. You'd then qualify for the 18%/28% rate of CGT on gains within your basic rate band and also potentially Entrepreneurs relief.

The downside to this is that any purchaser is very likely to look for a discount in the value of the company to reflect the fact that the company has an unrealised tax liability.

This means you won't get anywhere near as much for the shares as you would if you sold the assets personally.

If you can't retain profits in the company

The benefit of the company is that it has a lower rate of tax than you do personally. If you extract cash from the company you then incur a personal tax charge which eliminates much of the benefit of using the company.

So, if you hold personally you may suffer a 40% or 45% tax charge (as well as National Insurance if you're a trader).

If you hold via a company, the company may suffer a tax charge of 20% and you would suffer an effective tax rate at 25% on extraction of dividends.

When you take into account the other drawbacks of using a company, including the higher accounting and filing fees, extra admin etc the benefits may not be worthwhile.

If you need to make significant pension contributions

You may find it better to trade personally if you need to make large pension contributions.

Your ability to make pension contributions and get tax relief on them now depend on the level of your earned income. Therefore if you're trading personally you could potentially make a pension contribution of the amount of your net profit,(subject to the usual rules regarding the annual and lifetime pension limits).

You'd be taxed at 40%/45% but the pension would qualify for tax relief.

If you use a company, the company would be taxed on the profits generated. In order to make a large pension contribution you would need to have significant earned income.

Dividend income is not classed as earned income, and therefore you would need to extract cash as salary/bonus to use this as a 'base' for your pension contribution.

The downside to this is that you'd be looking at NIC charges on you (although only at 2% above the upper earnings limit) and on the company.

The company would pay NIC at 13.8% on the full amount of the bonus, although it would be tax deductible.

In this case the salary payment could in itself reduce the benefit of using a company significantly. The company may still have the edge but it would be more marginal,and when you take other issues into account... well that's up to you.

CHAPTER 4
HOW MUCH SALARY IN 2015/2016?

Dividends are usually the preferred way to extract cash from a company. This is now especially the case, as the higher and marginal rates of corporation tax are being reduced (thus reducing the tax benefit of paying a salary).

However, for many small company owners it will generally make sense to pay a salary equal to the employee's national insurance earnings threshold (£8,060 for 2015/16).

This will be tax free for the director because there is no income tax or employee's national insurance.

Furthermore, the salary will be a tax deductible expense for the company resulting in a corporation tax saving of £1,612 (£8,060 x 20%).

So a small salary is even better than tax free, it produces a tax cashback for the company!

Employer's national insurance kicks in on salaries over £8,060, so providing the salary is less than this there would be no Employer's NIC to pay.

Optimal Salaries for all Company Owners?

This is not necessarily the optimal salaries for ALL company owners. For some, the optimal salary will be affected by how much income the director has from others sources and how much money is being extracted from the company.

In many cases a salary of £8,000 is used. As well as being a nice round number - there is no national insurance to worry about and often no income tax.

Employer's and employee's national insurance kicks in when your salary exceeds £8,060 and income tax usually kicks in when your income exceeds £10,600.

A salary of £8,000 could escape all three taxes.

Although using a salary of £8,000 is ideal for the purposes of this guide – it is not necessarily the optimal salary for every company owner.

However, whether we use a salary of £8,000 or £8,060 or £10,600 will probably not make a huge amount of difference to the average business owner.

CHAPTER 5
WAYS TO REDUCE CORPORATION TAX

Reducing corporation tax isn't like reducing capital gains tax.

There's not a whole host of reliefs and exemptions that you can plough through to see if any apply.

Many of the reduction opportunities relate to reducing the profits. It sounds simple but achieving this in practice isn't straightforward.

Here's some of the top ways to reduce your corporation tax bill:

Make Pension Contributions

In terms of corporation tax relief for the company all employer contributions to registered pension schemes can in principle attract tax relief without limit (ie they're not restricted by the employees annual allowance).

However just as for any other expenses, pension contributions need to be incurred wholly and exclusively for the purposes of the trade to qualify for a tax deduction.

The Revenue view on this is that if an employee is not connected with the employer then contributions would usually qualify for relief on the basis that the payments were for a business purpose. If the employee is connected to the employer (eg a director in the company) the position is less straightforward.

Directors in small companies have significant flexibility as regards how to extract cash from a company, and making substantial pension contributions with only a low salary is a very tax efficient method of extraction.

In order for the company to qualify for a tax deduction (as stated above) the contribution needs to be wholly and exclusively for the trade.

So unless there's a non business purpose the pension contribution would be allowable. One of the ways that the Revenue can argue there is a non business purpose is where there is a substantial pension/salary package in relation to the services provided. HMRC have stated:

'...One situation where all or part of a contribution may not have been paid wholly & exclusively for the purposes of the trade is where the level of the remuneration package is excessive for the value of the work undertaken by that individual for the employer...'

If you can show that the contribution & salary package paid is in line with what would have been made for an unconnected employee in a similar situation it should qualify for tax relief.

You would therefore need to raise an argument that any salary & pension contributions were incurred by the company wholly and exclusively for the purposes of the trade and there was no non-business motive.

So in essence when looking at the tax deduction of the pension contribution in the company the key issue is the size of the remuneration package from the company when compared to the value of the work undertaken by that individual.

As always it's a question of fact, but the level of salary and pension would need to be reviewed as part of a total remuneration package as well as the duties/services provided.

Capital allowances

For small companies the new capital allowance regime is very generous. When calculating the profits for accounting purposes any capital expenditure is excluded.

So any assets you buy don't reduce your profits and therefore don't affect the amount of corporation tax on those profits. Instead assets are held on the balance sheet.

The reasoning behind this is that the capital expenditure benefits a business for years to come (ie an 'enduring benefit') and is not just restricted to the current accounting period.

However the tax provisions provide for separate corporation tax relief.

It was announced by the Chancellor that there will be an increase in the Annual Investment Allowance to £500,000 until 31 December 2015.

This applies to 'plant & machinery' expenditure. There are other allowances that apply eg for cars etc.

Plant & machinery will include many assets that are purchased for the purpose of a trade excluding cars and property (unless the property expenditure is directly related to the setting for the trade).

In recent years the rate has moved from £50,000 to £100,000 down to £25,000 and now up to £500,000.

HMRC have now issued guidance notes which say that this is a temporary increase and that the rate will drop to £200,000 after 1 January 2016.

The allowance is allocated based on the date of expenditure and the allowance for an accounting period which straddles the date of the rate change is pro-rated accordingly.

Writing down allowances at 18%/ 8% will be available on the amount exceeding the entitlement to Annual Investment Allowance.

You should therefore carefully review the capital expenditure on the balance sheet and assess whether you'll get capital allowances to reduce corporation tax.

Provisions

A provision made in accounts is the recognition of an expense or liability the timing or amount of which is uncertain. So it's essentially getting a tax deduction for expenditure before you've incurred it.

A provision made in accounts will only be allowable if:

☐ The business is under a present legal or constructive obligation to make the payments.

☐ The obligation is as a result of a past event, and

☐ it is probable that there will be a ' transfer of economic benefits' arising from the obligation. (ie the company will incur a cost).

Example of provisions that are allowable for tax purposes (as stated by the Revenue) include:

☐ in the period of sale for the cost of work under a warranty which a trader gives on the sale of merchandise (or under consumer protection legislation),

☐ for commission refundable by an insurance intermediary on the lapse of a policy where the commission is recognised as income at the inception of the policy,

☐ by builders for rectification work, including retentions up to the level that these have been recognised as income within accounts,

☐ for future maintenance of plant and machinery

Home expenses

The home is used by many companies and could be where the company actually carries out it's activities (eg a one man consultancy company).

Even if the company carries on most of its business elsewhere it is still entitled to a corporation tax deduction for the part of the household expenses provided that there are times when part of the home is used solely for business purposes.

Many of the bills for household expenses cover both business and private use. The part of the cost attributable to business use is allowable for tax purposes. It would then need to be recharged to the company for the company to qualify for a corporation tax deduction (eg by also crediting it to a directors loan account).

You clearly need to apportion any expenses between private and business use. the types of things you may consider here are:

☐ Area: what proportion is used for business purposes?

☐ Usage: how much is consumed? (eg where there is a metered supply such as electricity)

☐ Time: how long is it used for business purposes

There are of course lots of other tax deductions that you could consider. Some of the key lesser known ones include incidental costs of loan finance for companies and double tax relief. We look at these shortly.

CHAPTER 6
FINANCING A NEW COMPANY TAX EFFICIENTLY

When a new company is set up it's usually the case that cash needs to be transferred to it for the purchase of stock, materials, to cover running costs or to purchase property.

There are two main ways that this can be structured.

Firstly it could be as an equity injection - which usually means a purchase of share capital.

Alternatively it could be via debt. There is a lot of 'middle ground' here with funding options that are partly debt or partly equity, but this is the main distinction.

Why debt is often best

Very often Entrepreneurs transfer the cash to the company and leave it outstanding on loan account (ie the company owes the Entrepreneur the funds). In terms of bookkeeping the entry would be Dr Cash, Cr Creditors.

By having the cash structured as a loan this means that the shareholder can extract the cash from the company as they wish free of income tax and national insurance. This is because you can class extractions up to the initial funding as a repayment of a loan and therefore tax free.

You could charge interest to the company on the loaned funds if you wished.

This interest would typically be tax deductible for the company, but would be taxed on you personally (but would not be subject to national insurance).

For many this is a very attractive method of financing the new company. You can usually finance it with as much debt as you wish. There are provisions that apply an arms length basis where one party if outside the scope of UK tax (eg where the investor is non resident), however for UK residents the restrictions are minimal.

One of the main disadvantages is if the company is making losses and is to be wound up.

The tax implications of debts can be complex. Most debts are classed as simple debts, and as such there is no gain on the disposal of the debt but similarly there is no loss if the debt becomes irrevocable. Therefore there would be no tax relief in this case for the loss of the loan funding in the company.

However there are special rules that apply where a loan is made to a trader. In this case the tax legislation allows special loss relief. In order to qualify the loan:

☐ must have been for money,

☐ must have been made, to a borrower resident in the UK; and

☐ must have been used wholly for the purposes of the borrower's trade, or, provided that the trade is actually carried on subsequently, for the purposes of setting it up. Loans made where the borrower never commences a trade will not qualify.

☐ must not be between spouses or between companies in the same group

☐ must not be assigned

If these conditions are satisfied a capital loss can be treated as arising at the date of the claim.

Therefore in principle, providing any loan was made to your company for the purposes of carrying on a trade it should be possible to ensure that the debt that is irrevocable is classed as a capital loss.

Note that if the company was an investment company (eg a property investment company) no tax relief would be available.

This loss is a capital loss and as such can only be offset against capital gains, not income. Therefore if you realized a gain on the disposal of an asset (eg shares, property etc) the loss could be offset. This can be offset against any capital gains in the current year, as well as future years.

What is the position with equity/share capital financing?

Investing cash as share capital is treated as part of the base cost of the shares for tax purposes. Therefore if the company is wound up this would usually crystallise a capital loss equivalent to the original cost (assuming no proceeds).

However, if the shares were unquoted and if they were subscribed for directly from the company it would be possible to treat the loss as an income loss. For many this would be most attractive as it would allow the loss to be offset against other income such as employment or dividend income.

By contrast if the initial funding was as a loan account you'd be looking at a capital loss at best.

Of course the downside with acquiring share capital is that it would not allow an opportunity for the tax free extraction of cash from the company.

You'd be looking at a dividend extraction with an effective 25% tax charge for higher rate taxpayers (although basic rate taxpayers wouldn't suffer any further income tax).

CHAPTER 7
USING A DIRECTORS LOAN ACCOUNT TO REDUCE TAX

A directors loan account can be very attractive in reducing UK tax.

Essentially it applies where the company owes you money. It's shown as a creditor in the accounts and you can extract funds from this as and when you choose free of income tax and national insurance.

Where you owe the company money there are some nasty avoidance rules which can mean that the company has to pay a 25% tax charge and you are also subject to tax on the interest free or low interest element.

These provisions though don't apply where the loan is from you to the company. You can therefore make the loan interest free or have it as a full commercial interest bearing loan. Whatever the position the loan repayments are still free of tax for you.

Note though if it's an interest bearing loan the interest element will be treated separately. The interest would be allowed as a tax deduction under the loan relationship provisions (effectively giving you a corporation tax deduction). However it would then be subject to income tax in your hands.

When will a directors loan account arise?

It will occur whenever you transfer any asset or undertake services for the company and do not receive full consideration.

If you therefore transferred a car to the company which was valued at £5,000, you may not take any funds from the company to represent the £5,000 value. In this case you could either show this as a debt from the company or simply as a form of capital contribution by you.

Therefore the company would hold an asset at £5,000 and would either show a credit to loan account of £5,000 or a capital credit to the shareholders funds of £5,000. If a debt is established it allows the repayment to be made in the future free of tax.

It's for this reason that in many cases a sale - rather than a gift may be preferred. What you will have to beware of though is if you gift business assets you can often claim gift relief to defer any capital gain arising on the transfer.

However gift relief is restricted or even eliminated where some proceeds are received.

You therefore need to be very careful when deciding whether to sell for full consideration or to gift for nil consideration.

One of the key occasions when a directors loan account often arises is on the incorporation of a business. This simply means that the business is transferred to a company.

In this case, the business owner could sell the business to the company for full market value. They'd pay capital gains tax on the transfer at 18%/28% or 10% if Entrepreneurs Relief was available.

The proceeds could be left outstanding if it did not have the immediate funds and the shareholders/directors could then extract free of income tax as and when they chose.

They'd therefore potentially suffer an immediate 10% CGT charge (if Entrepreneurs Relief applied) but save income tax at up 45%.

If they didn't want to suffer any CGT charge on the transfer they could claim gift relief. However by gifting the business no loan account would be established. Often business owners will gift part of the business and sell the remainder a full value.

Use could always be made of the annual exemption. So for instance an asset valued at £100,000 but with a £20,000 gain could be put into joint names of a husband and wife and transferred to the company.

The gain would be offset by the annual CGT exemptions and the £100,000 could then be extracted free of tax.

Any transfer of assets to a company should therefore always be considered in terms of the potential impact on the loan account. If you can also arrange for a tax free transfer into the company you've achieved a 'double whammy' in tax terms as it'll be completely free of tax.

CHAPTER 8
MAXIMISING TAX RELIEF ON THE PURCHASE OF BUSINESS PREMISES

When you buy a business property this is classed as an asset for tax purposes. This means that you won't obtain tax relief for the cost of the property purchase as it is 'capital' expenditure for both tax & accounting purposes.

As such the property cost is held on your balance sheet as a 'fixed asset'.

This is completely different from the case of a property trader. A property trader buys and sells property as its main business. As such the property is not an 'asset' instead it is more like trading stock, and the cost of property isn't reflected on the balance sheet but is deducted when calculating the taxable profit of the business.

This difference is crucial as it means that businesses buying business premises won't be entitled to any tax relief for the cost of buying the property as it is capital expenditure.

Note that the 'cost' of the property not only includes the actual acquisition cost of the property, but also other costs involved in the purchase (eg stamp duty and conveyancing fees).

You will eventually get tax relief for the costs of buying the property but this will be when the property is sold. At this point any uplift in value from the cost of purchase would be classed as a capital gain and potentially subject to tax.

You may not however sell the property for a number of years, and if the costs of buying the property aren't allowable immediately what tax relief can you get on the actual purchase?

Well, your options for obtaining tax relief are limited. The main deductions are listed below:

Interest and finance costs

Finance costs are deductible from trading profits generally on the same basis as they are deducted in the accounts.

Deductions for finance costs

Purchasing property will give rise to a number of legal and other professional costs.

When you purchase business property this would give rise to a number of costs which may not be deductible from your taxable income. Generally these costs would be of a capital nature and can't be deducted from profits for tax purposes.

In such cases you need to identify those expenses which are associated directly with the borrowing and to exclude any expenses incurred in connection with the acquisition of the property.

It's essential to make the allocation as any legal and professional fees that are part of the funding exercise can be deducted from taxable income. This is under the deduction for 'incidental costs of obtaining finance or repaying a loan'.

The costs normally allowable include:

☐ Legal and professional expenses for negotiating the loan and preparing the documents.

☐ Underwriting commissions, brokerage and introduction fees.

☐ Land Registry fees, search fees and valuer's fees incurred in connection with the security for the loan.

☐ Commitment fees for an undertaking to make a loan available.

☐ Commissions for guaranteeing a loan.

☐ The costs of 'rolling over', extending, replacing, varying the terms of, or changing the security on, an existing loan.

So you'd be able to offset costs such as:

Interest payable

- Premium/discount on redemption of the loan
- Costs of obtaining loan finance
- Abortive expenses in connection with a loan facility that it never drawn
- Termination costs of repaying loan finance
- Any other payments made under the terms of a loan including payments to reimburse a lenders costs or vary the terms of a loan

Given the wide scope of the deduction for traders on finance costs it makes sense for any fees to be allocated as much as possible to the funding of the building.

If you do this the fees will then be deductible. If the finance is substantial it's therefore worthwhile liasing with any professionals supplying their services in relation to a property acquisition to ensure they allocate an appropriate proportion of their fees to the funding exercise.

Remember though that the actual legal and other costs of the purchase won't be deductible. It will only be the funding element that is deductible.

Interest deduction

The deduction for interest will be one of the most significant deductions in many property purchases. The trader would get tax relief for this given it's incurred 'wholly & exclusively' for the purposes of the trade. Note that companies have a separate set of rules that apply to how interest is taxed/deducted on them. These are the 'loan relationship' provisions. Generally though although the rules differ they still get tax relief against their profits.

If you have excess finance/interest costs this would be offset against other income and then carried forward/back.

Capital allowances

The other main opportunity for tax relief is by claiming capital allowances.

Capital allowances are available on a capital expenditure incurred by a person carrying on a 'qualifying activity' on plant & machinery that was acquired for that purpose.

A trade is a qualifying activity.

Allowances are fixed at 18% of the cost per year (after April 2012) but you'll be likely to get 100% relief on expenditure up to £500,000 to 31 December 2015. After this the threshold reduces to £200,000.

It can therefore prove very tax efficient to carefully ascertain the costs that will qualify for plant & machinery allowances (certainly at the 100% rate, but also at the 18% plant & machinery rate).

The problem is in ascertaining exactly what is plant/machinery and what is simply the structure. The former is allowance whilst expenditure that relates to the building structure would not be allowable.

HMRC does provide a list of various types of expenditure which they regard as not being automatically excluded from a capital allowance claim. Some of the key items of expenditure include:

☐ Manufacturing or processing equipment; storage equipment (including cold rooms); display equipment; and counters, checkouts and similar equipment
☐ Cookers, washing machines, dishwashers, refrigerators and similar equipment; washbasins, sinks, baths, showers, sanitary ware and

similar equipment; and furniture and furnishings
- ☐ Sound insulation provided mainly to meet the particular requirements of the qualifying activity
- ☐ Computer, telecommunication and surveillance systems (including their wiring or other links)
- ☐ Refrigeration or cooling equipment
- ☐ Fire alarm systems; sprinkler and other equipment for extinguishing or containing fires
- ☐ Burglar alarm systems
- ☐ Strong rooms in bank or building society premises; safes
- ☐ Partition walls, where moveable and intended to be moved in the course of the qualifying activity
- ☐ Decorative assets provided for the enjoyment of the public in hotel, restaurant or similar trades
- ☐ Advertising hoardings; signs, displays and similar assets

Whether any of these would actually qualify would depend on whether they were actually required for the purposes of the trade.

You'll see that careful allocation of the costs of the purchase of a building can reap dividends. Capital allowances can be lost simply because of an inappropriate description or allocation of the amounts involved.

Many large companies take great care over this and ensure that the purchase consideration is allocated in the acquisition agreement to show the amounts allocated to the relevant qualifying expenditure (fire alarm, burglar alarm etc).

Remember the professional fees as well. Any fees that you can allocate to the capital allowance claim would also qualify for allowances. So the fees of mechanical and electrical engineers may well be linked to the installation of plant and would therefore qualify.

In some cases 40-50% of the purchase price of modern buildings are attributable to qualifying fixtures & equipment eligible for capital allowances.

Repairs after purchase

If you buy a property in a poor condition as a general rule you'll be able to deduct the costs of repairs. The fact that you bought the property not long before the repairs are made doesn't in itself make the repair a capital expense.

There are though occasions when HMRC may argue otherwise (ie that the expenditure is capital and therefore not deductible). This would include cases where you have an agreement to renovate the property or where there is a very substantial deduction as the property is in a dilapidated state.

Provisions for repairs

You can also deduct a repairs provision where you have a liability to pay for the work but payment hasn't been made at the year end. This would then reduce the taxable profits even though payment hasn't yet been made.

Note though you need to have incurred a liability to pay, and you won't therefore get a deduction for repairs that you think you may incur in the future.

CHAPTER 9
TRANSFERRING PROPERTY ASSETS OUT OF A COMPANY TAX EFFICIENTLY

A common scenario is for a company to hold both trading and investment assets. This could be because the shareholders have decided to use retained cash in the company to purchase investment properties or other investment assets (in the belief that this saves on the tax charge on extracting funds from the company).

Alternatively it may simply be the case that assets that were previously used for trading purposes (eg property) are now held as an investment.

This is usually fine until you start to think about the future disposal of either the property or the trade.

Taking a disposal of the trade, there would usually be no problem with this and the shareholders could consider a sale of the shares in the company. This can be very tax efficient and Entrepreneurs Relief will often reduce the tax rate to 10%.

However many purchasers will not want to buy a company complete with the property investment assets, and you would therefore need to think about extracting these from the company prior to a disposal.

In addition, having an investment asset in the company that is 'substantial' could prevent Entrepreneurs Relief from applying and the CGT rate could be increased to 28%.

It is usually therefore advised to separate the investment from the trading activities. How you actually do this without paying a fortune in tax though is another question.

A simple transfer of the property from the company to the shareholders or another company would be a disposal by the original company. As such a gain would arise based on the market value of the property (usually).

If the shareholders are UK resident the transfer at undervalue would also be taxed on them as though they had received a dividend. This would then be subject to income tax on the element of undervalue.

So all in all this is not really a good option.

Another option which may be preferable could be to consider a demerging of the existing company, with the separation of the trading and the investment activities.

There are specific tax provisions that provide for CGT reliefs on a demerger applicable to trading companies or the insolvency act could be used. The existing trading company could probably be liquidated during this process, and the assets split into newco's.

Under this the existing company is placed in liquidation and in essence the liquidator transfers the assets to newcos established by the shareholders, in exchange for the issue of shares to the shareholders(eg X Ltd & Yltd).

They could then dispose of the shares in X Ltd directly without the need to crystalize a gain on Y Ltd. This treatment can also apply for investment assets and the shares in X and Y Ltd would be treated as being owned for the same holding period as the existing trading company.

Therefore Newco X could receive the Investment property and Newco Y could receive the trading assets. The newcos would remain owned by the existing shareholders and they could then sell the trading company separately from the investment asset/company.

Note that these are all complex areas and should be looked at in some significant detail.

In terms of stamp duty if the shareholding proportions will be the same as they were for the current company (ie the owners would have exactly the same percentage shareholdings in X Ltd as they currently have in the trading company) it should be possible to avoid stamp duty on this transfer, although the anti avoidance provisions would need to be reviewed in detail.

The shareholders could then dispose of the shares in X Ltd or Y Ltd. A gain would arise and Entrepreneurs Relief could apply.

This would still represent a significant tax saving in many cases when compared with a company disposal of assets (although clearly the specific facts would need to be considered eg the base cost of shares/assets, any capital losses etc).

Therefore if you're looking at splitting an existing trading company a demerger could be considered. Note that ideally this should be done a significant period before a disposal of the shares to a third party purchaser, although if necessary the liquidation route may be considered for disposals shortly after the reorganisation.

CHAPTER 10
MAKING YOUR COMPANY INVESTOR READY
FOR EIS RELIEF

If you're looking to attract investors to your company, an added incentive for them will be if they can get tax relief on their investment. The key opportunity for relief will be under the Enterprise Investment Scheme ("EIS").

Tax Reliefs On Offer

There are five types of relief available under the EIS, relating to income tax, capital gains tax, loss relief, capital gains tax deferral relief and inheritance tax relief.

☐ Income tax relief is available for individuals who subscribe for new shares in an EIS qualifying company. The relief is available at 30 per cent of the cost of the shares up to £1M (for shares issued after 5 April 2012).

There is a carry back facility where shares subscribed in one tax year can be set against the income tax liability for the previous year. Relief cannot be carried forward.

☐ Capital gains tax will not be payable on any gain on the shares if they are held for a qualifying period (see below).

☐ If the shares are disposed of at a loss, the investor can elect that the loss (less any income tax relief already claimed) be set against any other income for that year, or the previous year, instead of being set against any capital gains.

☐ The payment of tax on a capital gain can be deferred where the gain is re-invested in the shares of an EIS qualifying company.

The deferral is available up to 1 year before or 3 years after the gain arose. There is no minimum or maximum value or holding period and it does not matter if the investor is connected with the company.

☐ Due to the interaction with Business Property Relief, shareholdings in companies that qualify for the EIS may fall outside the scope of the inheritance tax regime after two years.

Can The Investor Qualify?

☐ The shares issued to the investor must be paid up in full in cash on issue and must be "full risk" ordinary shares with no preferential rights to dividends, or to the company's assets on a winding up.

If the company puts in place any arrangements to protect the investors from the risks of investing in the company or for the purchase of the shares after the qualifying period, then the investor will not be able to benefit from the tax reliefs. Investors should note that the reliefs are only available for new issues of shares and not purchases.

☐ The shares must be held for three years from the date of issue, or three years from the date the qualifying trade started if this is after the shares are issued, for the income tax and capital gains tax reliefs to be available.

☐ An investor will not be eligible for income tax relief or capital gains tax exemption if he is connected with the company. An investor is deemed to be connected if he is a director (unless the business angel exemption applies - see below) or an employee of the company. This restriction applies if the investor was connected in the two year period prior to the shares being issued and three years after the issue.

☐ An exemption applies to directors who do not receive (and are not entitled to) any remuneration for holding the post.

☐ The "business angel" exemption applies to investors who subsequently become paid directors if:

o the investor is not connected to the company when the shares are issued and the later directorship is the only connection;

o the investor had not previously been involved in carrying on the trade the company is involved in; and

o the investor's pay as director is reasonable.

☐ An investor will also be connected if he alone or together with associates holds more than 30 per cent of the share capital (or share and loan capital taken together) or more than 30 per cent of the voting rights. or is entitled to more than 30 per cent of the assets of the company on a winding up.

☐ The shares must be subscribed for genuine commercial reasons and not for tax avoidance purposes.

Will The Company Qualify?

The company will have to satisfy the following key criteria:

☐ It must not be traded on the London Stock Exchange's Main Market or any other recognised stock exchange. The AIM and PLUS markets are not considered to be recognised exchanges and so a company listed on these markets may still qualify.

☐ The company must not be controlled by another company and there must not be arrangements in place for this to happen.

☐ If the company has subsidiaries it must own more than 50 per cent of each one (or 90 per cent in the case of a property management subsidiary).

☐ It must be a "small company" i.e. have gross assets of less than £15 million before the investment and £16 million afterwards for shares issued on or after 6 April 2012.

☐ It must be either a company carrying on a qualifying trade or the parent company of a trading group, but it must own 90 per cent of the subsidiary carrying on the qualifying trade.

☐ It must not raise more than £5m in any 12 month period from the three venture capital schemes (EIS, Corporate Venturing Scheme and Venture Capital Trusts).A lifetime limit has been introduced to cap the maximum amount it can raise under the venture capital schemes. This limit will be £12 million for most companies.

☐ The trade for which the money has been raised must be carried on wholly or mainly in the United Kingdom (this will be changed in the forthcoming Finance Act so that the company only requires a permanent UK establishment). Many trades qualify for the relief, although a company will not be eligible where more than 20 per cent of its activities are "excluded activities" (see below).

☐ The investment funds can be used for the purpose of preparing to carry on a trade (including research and development), but any such trade must start within 2 years of the shares being issued.

☐ The shares must be subscribed for genuine commercial reasons and not for tax avoidance purposes.

Excluded Activities

The following activities are excluded:

☐ Dealing in land, in commodities or futures in shares, securities or other financial instruments;

☐ Dealing in goods, other than in an ordinary trade of retail or wholesale distribution;

☐ Financial activities such as banking, insurance, money-lending, debt factoring, hire-purchase financing or any other financial activities;

☐ Leasing or letting assets on hire, except in the case of certain ship-chartering activities;

☐ Receiving royalties or licence fees (though if these arise from the exploitation of an intangible asset which the company itself has created, that is not an excluded activity);

☐ Providing legal or accountancy services;

☐ Property development;

☐ Farming or market gardening;

☐ Holding, managing or occupying woodlands, any other forestry activities or timber production;

☐ Shipbuilding;

☐ Coal production;

☐ Steel production;

☐ Operating or managing hotels or comparable establishments or managing property used as an hotel or comparable establishment;

☐ Operating or managing nursing homes or residential care homes, or managing property used as a nursing home or residential care home; and

☐ Providing services to another person where that person's trade consists, to a substantial extent, of excluded activities, and the person controlling that trade also controls the company providing the services.

Qualifying Requirements

The company must comply with the above criteria on an ongoing basis in order for investors to benefit from the tax reliefs for the three year qualifying period.

CHAPTER 11
QUALIFYING FOR THE NEW SEIS

The Government has launched a new Seed Enterprise Investment Scheme (SEIS) aimed at encouraging investment in very small, new companies. SEIS has many similarities with the Enterprise Investment Scheme (EIS), but there are significant differences.

Tax relief available under SEIS Income tax relief

☐ Individuals who make qualifying investments will benefit from income tax relief equal to 50 per cent of the amount invested.

However, the relief is subject to an annual subscription limit of £100,000 (ie, a maximum tax saving of £50,000). Investors can use the relief against their tax liability for the tax year in which they subscribe, the preceding tax year, or split the relief between the two years. Investment must be in subscription to new shares issued on or after 6 April 2012 until 5 April 2017.

Capital gains tax (CGT) reliefs

☐ Whenever an investment in shares benefits from income tax relief under SEIS, any disposal of those shares will also exempt from CGT, provided that the shares have been held for at least three years and the SEIS conditions have been met throughout that period.

☐ Chargeable gains arising on the disposal of other capital assets that are reinvested in SEIS shares qualify for a 50% exemption from CGT

☐ Where shares are sold at a loss, the allowable loss for CGT purposes is reduced to take account of any income tax received. In some circumstances, the allowable loss will be eligible to set against income.

Eligibility and conditions

Who can benefit?

☐ SEIS tax reliefs apply to qualifying investors who subscribe for relevant shares in qualifying companies where all the applicable conditions are satisfied.

Who is a qualifying investor?

☐ The investor must be an individual who is making the investment on his own behalf (though he may invest via a nominee).

☐ Neither the investor, nor any of his associates, may be an employee of the investee company/group at any time during the period from the issue of the relevant shares to the third anniversary of that issue, (referred to as "Period B" in the draft legislation).

☐ However, where a person is a director of a company, he will not count as an employee for this purpose.

Thus, an executive or non-executive director of a qualifying company can make SEIS investments.

However, unless he is an unpaid director, he may be able to make follow on investments under EIS. the rules are complex and, if this could be an issue, advice should be taken.

☐ The investor must not have a "substantial interest" in the investee company at any time during the period from incorporation of the investee company to the third anniversary of the issue, of the relevant shares (referred to as "Period A" in the draft legislation).

In summary, the investor must not alone or with his associates hold directly or indirectly, or be entitled to acquire, more than 30 per cent of the ordinary share capital; issued share capital or voting rights of the investee company; or any of its subsidiaries or be entitled to more than 30 per cent of the assets on a winding up.

What are relevant shares?

☐ Relevant shares are ordinary shares with no right to be redeemed, no preferential rights to assets on a winding up, and whose preferential rights to dividends (if any at all) comply with strict rules.

This includes not being dependent on a decision of the company, or the investor or any other person, and not being cumulative rights where unpaid dividends are carried forward for payment in a later year.

☐ The shares must be:

i. subscribed for wholly in cash and fully paid up when issued;

ii. issued to raise money for a qualifying business activity to be carried on by the issuing company or a 90 per cent subsidiary.

A qualifying business activity is carrying on of a new qualifying trade (see below); or preparing to carry on a new qualifying trade; or undertaking research and development from which it is intended to derive a new qualifying trade or benefit a "new qualifying trade".

☐ The concept a "new qualifying trade" is central to SEIS and includes the following features:

iii. the trade must be a qualifying trade (ie, one which does not include, wholly or to a substantial extent, excluded activities). The definition of "excluded activities" is the same for EIS and SEIS and includes activities such as dealing in land, certain property-backed trades (such as property development and farming) and certain financial trades;

iv. the trade must be less than two years old. If the trade in question was carried on by the relevant company, or by any other person, more than two years prior before the date of issue of the relevant shares, it will not count as a new qualifying trade; and vi. the trade must be the company/group's first trade. A trade will not be a new qualifying trade if, prior to its commencement, either the issuing company or one of its subsidiaries has carried on any other trade.

What is a qualifying company?

☐ The company must, if a single company, exist for the purpose of carrying on a new qualifying trade. If the company is the parent of a group, the group's business must not consist to a substantial extent (ie, 20 per cent or more) in non-qualifying activities (that is, trading activities which do not qualify for EIS or SEIS or non-trading activities).

☐ The company (or, if applicable, the group) must:

i. have gross assets which do not exceed £200,000 immediately before the relevant shares are issued;

ii. have fewer than 25 full-time equivalent employees when the relevant shares are issued.

☐ The company must not have raised funds under the EIS or Venture Capital Trust ("VCT") regimes before or on the day on which the relevant shares are issued for SEIS purposes.

☐ The company:

iii. must not be controlled by any other company (or any other company and any person connected with that other company);

iv. must not have any subsidiary which is not a "qualifying subsidiary" (broadly, a genuine subsidiary);

v. must have a permanent UK establishment;

vi. must be an unquoted company;

vii. must not, when the relevant shares are issued, be in "financial difficulty", under applicable European Commission guidelines.

For each of these conditions, the times for which they must be satisfied are slightly different.

☐ The qualifying business activity must be carried on by the issuing company, or a 90 per cent subsidiary and neither the company nor any of its 90 per cent subsidiaries may be a member of a partnership.

Additional applicable conditions

☐ Funds raised under SEIS must be spent within 3 years for a qualifying business activity.

☐ There is a maximum limit of £150,000, which may be raised by a company under SEIS; this is not an annual threshold but a maximum amount per company.

☐ SEIS reliefs must be claimed and an investor will not be entitled to make a claim for relief, until the issuing company has provided him with a "compliance certificate". The issuing company is not permitted to apply to HM Revenue & Customs for a compliance certificate until:

i. at least 70 per cent of the money invested has been spent; and
ii. the new qualifying trade of the issuing company, or its 90 per cent subsidiary, has been carried on for at least four months.

☐ There are a number of anti-avoidance provisions (including a requirement that the investment be undertaken for genuine commercial reasons and a prohibition on terms of issue such as protection against the ordinary risks of investment including, for example, anti-dilution rights).

Loss of tax reliefs

☐ If the investor effects a disposal of the relevant shares (which includes granting a call option or receiving a put option) before the third anniversary of the date of issue, income tax relief may be clawed back in whole or in part and any chargeable gain will be subject to CGT in the normal way.

☐ Complex rules, similar to those in the EIS code in relation to "value received" by the investor, mean that where the investor receives value from the issuing company or one of its subsidiaries, unless the receipt is an "excluded payment" or an "insignificant" amount, income tax relief may be clawed back in whole or in part.

CHAPTER 12
SHOULD PROPERTY DEVELOPERS USE A SEPARATE COMPANY FOR EACH DEVELOPMENT

Some of the big name property developers use separate companies for each property development. In this chapter we look at whether this is beneficial in terms of reducing your tax UK taxes.

How it works

Some of the big property development companies typically structure their developments as:

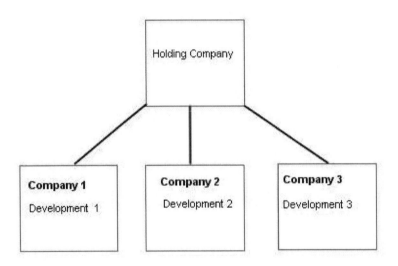

The shareholders own an interest in the holding company and the holding company owns the shares in the underlying subsidiary companies.

There are a number of reasons for doing this:

Sale of shares

If each of the developments was undertaken in the same company (the holding company for instance) and the shareholders wanted to sell the who development onto a third party seller, this would make it much more difficult.

They couldn't just sell the shares in the company to the purchaser as the company would also contain the other development trades which the purchaser would not be buying.

If the company was to sell just development 1 from the company this would crystallise either a capital gain in the holding company based on the proceeds received less the costs of the development or it would be taxed as trading income.

The latter would permit a wider range of deductions including interest on funds to finance the development. This would then be taxed in the company at rates of up to 20%. The extraction of cash as a dividend by the shareholders would then incur an income tax charge on them personally.

So what to do?

Well, this is one of the reasons why the developments are separated into different companies.

If you adopted the structure as shown in the above diagram, the holding company could just sell the shares in Company 1.

The key advantage of this is that the holding company could potentially qualify for an exemption for capital gains purposes on the disposal of the shares. This is by virtue of the substantial shareholdings exemption.

Note that this applies providing the companies are involved in a property development trade (not investment).

The shareholders would still be subject to income on the extraction of cash as a dividend from the holding company but the avoidance of corporation tax on any capital gain would be a key incentive to using separate companies.

Joint ventures

Another advantage of establishing the different developments within different companies is that it's easier to bring in other associated partners. Partners are often brought in on certain development and they can be brought into the development by receiving share capital.

This would then given them a share of the profits of that particular development.

If the trades were all held within one company giving the partners shares in the main company would not be an option unless the shares were split into different classes.

Asset protection

By keeping the developments within different companies they are keeping them legally separate. Therefore this reduces the risk of one development being held liable for the debts of another development.

There are therefore some advantages to keeping the companies separate. Note that as the companies would all form a group for tax purposes they could each surrender losses and transfer capital gains within the group free of tax.

The key disadvantage to using a group of companies such as this is that it will increase the number of companies for associated companies purposes.

Companies are associated where they are under common control.

In the example above you'd have 3 associated companies. Where there are associated companies this reduces the corporation tax bands accordingly. So if there are three associated companies this would reduce the small company band from £300,000 to £100,000 and the main corporation tax band from £1.5M to £500,000.

This used to be more of a problem than it is now as the small company band and main band are being aligned.

Therefore using multiple companies for the different developments could be a good idea.

CHAPTER 13
WHY IT CAN MAKE SENSE FOR PROPERTY INVESTORS TO USE A HOLDING COMPANY

Ensuring that you have the correct structure set up for your property investment or property development activities can be half the battle in terms of minimising taxes.

Many property developers hold property developments via separate companies.

Whilst this can be attractive in terms of limiting the liabilities you need to look carefully at the tax implications.

In particular there's a big difference between this structure:

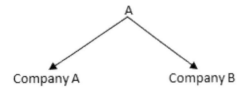

And this:

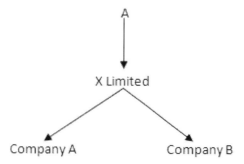

In the first instance the individual owns the two property investment companies personally. In other words he owns 100% of the shares in A and 100% of the shares in B.

In the second instance the same individual owns 100% of the shares in X Limited. This then owned 100% of the shares in Company A and Company B.

Why use a holding company?

Many property investors structure their property investment activities as in the first example. Aside from the issue of whether a corporate structure is the best option for property investors if they do opt for a corporate structure the first structure can have some significant disadvantages - particularly if one of the companies
realises a capital loss (perhaps more likely given the current economic slowdown).

In order to transfer assets between the companies tax efficiently they would need to form a group for capital gains tax purposes.

This effectively means that a company forms a group with its 75% subsidiaries and 75% subsidiaries of those subsidiaries, and so on.

It is also required that there is at least an effective 51% ownership.

Therefore if both A & B were owned under a holding company such as X Ltd (with the shares owned by you), this would form a group.

The key benefit of a group for capital gains tax purposes is that it can transfer an asset with a latent loss tax free to a company with a capital gain, and then crystallise the loss in the gain company.

Provided the gain crystallises in the same accounting period as the loss, or in a later accounting period to which the loss is carried forward, the tax charge is only on the net gain, if any.

If there is no capital gains group there would be no option to offset losses between the two companies. So you could have a situation where Company A may realise a loss, and Company B a gain on a disposal. In this case the loss from Company A couldn't be offset against the gain in Company B.

If there was a group the loss could be used.

The group structure also allows the transfer of any rental losses between the two companies which would not apply if there was no group.

Disadvantage of using a holding company

 If the companies are owned directly by the shareholder there is always the option of selling the shares in the company rather than the underlying property. This would then be taxed at 18% or 28% on the individual (or even exempt if the shareholder was non UK resident).

The holding company could sell the shares in the underlying company but this would crystallise a capital gain in the holding company. If the subsidiary was an investment company the substantial shareholding exemption would not be available.

This may not though be an issue if a sale of the shares was not on the cards.

In this case the proceeds would be transferred free of tax to the holding company, and could be extracted by the shareholder with the same tax implications as if he held the company directly.

CHAPTER 14
DOES IT STILL MAKE SENSE TO RENT PROPERTY TO YOUR TRADING COMPANY?

Many business owners own business premises personally and let their company trade through the premises. The main advantage to this is in terms of selling the business property separately from the business.

If the property was held by the company you would need to arrange for a disposal by the company. This would then crystallise a capital gain on the property in the company (taxed at 20%) and there could also be a tax charge on the extraction of the proceeds by the shareholders.

Holding property personally avoids these problems, and the property owners (usually also the company shareholders) can sell the property directly.

Rent or not?

The property owners have a choice whether to charge rent to the company or not. If they do, the rent would be tax deductible for the company but would be subject to income tax for the property owners (at their marginal rate of income tax, ie 20% or 40%/45%).

Unfortunately along with many other changes from April 2008, the changes to the tax relief for disposal of businesses included a tax 'penalty' for cases where a market rental is charged.

Entrepreneurs Relief and the payment of rent

Entrepreneurs Relief replaces Taper Relief on the disposal of businesses/shares in personal trading companies after 5 April 2008.

In the case of a property owner ('A') who holds business property in his own name which is used for the purpose of his trading company ('X Ltd'), A would only be entitled to Entrepreneurs Relief on a disposal of the business premises if it qualified as an 'associated disposal'.

There are various conditions to be satisfied however essentially the property would need to be used by X Ltd for the purposes of the trade for the year before disposal.

In addition A would need to sell the shares in X Ltd and the disposal of the premises would need to be part and parcel of his withdrawal from the business.

Therefore A could only claim Entrepreneurs Relief against the gain on a disposal of the property if he also sold shares in X Ltd.

Assuming though that this restriction is met there is a further restriction.

The legislation also states that where:

☐ only part of the assets are used for the trade

☐ the property is used for trading purposes for only part of the ownership period

☐ rent is payable from the company to the owners only a 'just and reasonable' amount of Entrepreneurs Relief is due.

The legislation defines this 'just and reasonable' adjustment in the context of rent by saying that you have to have regard to 'the extent to which any rent paid is less than the amount which would be payable in the open market for the use of the assets'.

Therefore if a full market rental was paid no Entrepreneurs Relief would be due, whereas if no rent was paid full Entrepreneurs may be due.

The thinking here is that if the property was only available on the payment of rent it is effectively an investment in the hands of A rather than being employed solely for the purposes of the business.

There can therefore be a significant disadvantage to charging a market rental to your trading company as it could prove very costly on a future disposal.

Where Entrepreneurs Relief does apply it reduces the gain on the property to 10%. If no Entrepreneurs Relief was due CGT would be charged at 28%. On a gain of £500,000 on a property disposal, renting the property to the company could therefore potentially lead to an additional CGT charge of £90,000.

What advantages are there to charging rent?

Any plan to charge rent to the company would need to carefully weigh up any tax advantages of charging the rent with the possible restriction in Entrepreneurs Relief on a future disposal.

In many cases there may be no advantages to charging rent, however here are some of the cases where charging rent could be beneficial in terms of reducing tax:

☐ Where you have a spouse who has little activity within a business, the ability to extract cash in the form of rental in their name (to utilise their personal allowance and basic rate tax band) could be advantageous.

However, now that HMRC have announced a temporary suspension of the attack on income shifting this makes this less important.

Nevertheless it could be important in the future

☐ Although rental income is subject to income tax in the hands of the property owner it is not subject to national insurance.

This makes is preferable to extracting salary or bonus which is subject to employers and employees NIC. However, in many companies the remuneration approach is to pay small salaries to the shareholders and extract the rest by way of dividends. There is therefore no national insurance liability and this other possible benefit of paying rent may not be applicable

If the property owners had taken out a substantial loan to purchase the property the interest deduction could substantially reduce the rental profit.

The company would get a tax deduction for the rental saving tax at 20% but the property may only suffer a very low tax charge on the rental profits. If no rent was charged the interest may not obtain any tax relief.

Therefore any decision whether to charge rent to your trading company needs to be carefully considered. If a disposal is on the cards in the future the restriction in Entrepreneurs Relief could easily outweigh any benefits of charging rent.

CHAPTER 15
UK CORPORATION TAX PLANNING IF YOU LEAVE THE UK

If you trade via a UK company, the general rule is that it would be subject to UK corporation tax even if the controlling directors or shareholders were non UK resident.

As the company is a UK company it is classed as UK resident and is subject to UK corporation tax at 20%.

Although the UK company would still be subject to UK corporation tax if the shareholders were non resident, this doesn't mean that there aren't opportunities for UK tax planning.

Extracting cash from the company

In terms of actually extracting cash from the company this could be easily achieved by extracting dividends.

If the shareholders are non resident they are taxed on dividends only to the extent that there is UK tax deducted at source. UK dividends have a notional tax credit of 1/9 attached, and the net effect is that non residents can receive dividends free of UK income tax.

Therefore they can extract profits from the company free of UK tax, however these profits will still have been subject to corporation tax in the UK company.

If the aim is to reduce the corporation tax on the company profits you would need to look at additional options.Note, however that in the 2015 Summer Budget it was announced that from April 2016 this tax credit will be abolished and the tax regime for dividends will be changed. We look at this later in the book.

Salary/Bonus

The simplest way is to pay salary/bonuses to employees/directors.

The salary/bonus would not be subject to income tax or NIC provided the directors were non resident and carried out the duties of employment overseas (aside from any incidental UK duties).

The company is permitted a tax deduction for all expenses incurred "wholly and exclusively" for the purposes of the trade.

Therefore in order for the company to substantiate a tax deduction for salary or bonus payments it would need to be linked to a benefit received by the company and for the purposes of its trade.

This usually means that the salary/bonus payments need to be related to:

• Genuine services provided by the employees/directors to the company, and

• Calculated at an arms length rate for those services.

Essentially you would want to be able to argue that the company would make payments even if the employees/directors were otherwise unconnected with the company (ie not shareholders).

You could for instance look at paying both a market value salary for the duties undertaken by non resident directors as well as a bonus arrangement related to their specific fields of responsibility.

Offshore company

The other option would be to use an offshore structure, particularly an offshore company and recharge amounts to the UK company.

In terms of the company itself you would need to ensure:

1) It was controlled and managed from overseas. There should be no

issue with this if the controlling directors and shareholders are non resident.

2) It had no UK trade (as even if non resident, profits from a UK trade could still be within the scope of UK tax). The location of the trade is usually where the key revenue generating activities are undertaken.

The simplest way to use an offshore company is for the directors to provide services via this to the UK company.

This is a form of service company. Similar considerations apply as above (ie in terms of transfer pricing) and you would need to ensure that the rates charged were at market levels for the services provided.

The offshore company would receive the receipts free of UK and local tax. The UK company would obtain a tax deduction for the payments.

If you were looking to transfer part of the trade to an offshore company, this could avoid UK tax. The offshore company would recharge for the services to the UK company which would be free of tax in the offshore company. A BVI or IOM company is often used for this purpose.

HMRC usually accept that a service company used to employ staff, own or lease business premises or provide other administrative services is genuine assuming that the company recharges the UK co at an appropriate mark up (eg 10-15%).

Another option would be to use an offshore holding company.

You'd achieve this by using a share for share exchange to place the new offshore company as the holding company of the UK company.

A management recharge from the UK to the offshore company would be deductible for corporation tax purposes but again you would need to ensure that it related to genuine services provided by the offshore co to the UK company. A management recharge of

100% of the profits for instance would not be acceptable.

Goodwill

An important issue on a transfer of any aspect of the trade would be whether there was a transfer of goodwill from the UK company.

The transfer of the trade from the UK company to the offshore company would be a disposal for capital gains purposes. This isn't a specific rule that applies to transfers to offshore companies but rather is a general rule that applies on the transfer of any assets out of a company.

Therefore irrespective of the disposal consideration that is actually transferred from the offshore company to the UK any capital gain in the UK company would be based on the market value of the assets transferred.

You would therefore need to value the assets that were transferred to the offshore company. This would include plant/machinery, any land or property but usually goodwill is the largest asset transferred.

However, if the value of the goodwill is represented by the personal services carried out the directors they may be able to argue that it is effectively personal goodwill. If this was the case they may be able to argue that there was no disposal for CGT purposes.

Aside from this a transfer of back office operations with a recharge to the UK company would usually be acceptable.

In terms of actually transferring the revenue generating activities the best option could be to undertake new activities in the offshore company where there could be no argument of a transfer of goodwill. The profits would then arise free of UK tax in the offshore company.

Distribution

The other key tax issue on the transfer of the trade overseas is that the transfer would also be treated as a distribution (ie a dividend) to the shareholders given that they have extracted value from the company.

The amount of the distribution would be the undervalue at which the trade was transferred.

Note though that non UK residents are only charged to UK income tax on dividends to the extent that tax was deducted at source. Given that there would be no tax deducted at source it may be possible to avoid income tax on the distribution.

The alternative would be for the offshore company to pay the full market value to the UK company for the trade.

There would then be no distribution on the transfer but the shareholders could extract the cash as non residents free of further income tax.

Anti Avoidance Rules

As from April 2013 the new Statutory Residence Test also introduces a "temporary non residence" rule that will apply to dividends.

The new rules state that if you become non resident and extract dividends from a UK company which represent profits that were accumulated whilst you were UK resident, you would need to be non resident for more than five complete tax years to avoid income tax being charged on the dividends when you return.

CHAPTER 16
TRANSFERRING YOUR UK COMPANY OVERSEAS TO AVOID UK TAX

Some of the UK's largest companies have transferred their operations overseas. In this chapter we look at how a UK company can 'migrate' overseas tax efficiently and the tax benefits in doing so.

There are a lot of different ways of structuring the move overseas, however the most drastic, and also the most effective in terms of minimising ongoing taxes is to relocate the holding/principal company overseas. This is known as a company migration.

The benefit of this is that the company would be exempt from UK tax on overseas profits as well as UK and overseas capital gains.

UK trading profits would still be subject to UK tax, however for companies with overseas operations the tax benefits of moving abroad can be substantial. Allied to this is the fact that they can frequently transfer operations abroad to avoid having a UK taxable presence in any case.

You can then establish the company in a low tax jurisdiction such as Ireland or Cyprus with corporation tax rates as low as 12.5%/10%.

Where you have a UK incorporated company there are two main ways that it can effectively migrate:

☐ Firstly it can become non UK resident by virtue of having treaty residence overseas.

☐ Secondly, you can look to some fancy restructuring to interpose a new offshore holding company

Treaty residence

This is the only real way to completely migrate.

If the UK company is resident in an overseas country by virtue of the overseas country rules you would then need to look at the double tax treaty to see which country the company is 'treaty resident' in.

For companies the standard double tax treaty decides the question of treaty residence by looking at which country the effective control is exercised from. If it is the UK, the company would be UK treaty resident. If it's controlled from overseas it could be classed as treaty resident overseas. Any company that is treaty resident overseas is classed as non UK resident for UK tax purposes.

This therefore means that the transfer of control overseas under the scope of a double tax treaty could cause a UK exit charge on the migration (as the company would be deemed to be non UK resident).

Anyone owning a UK company and planning to move overseas would therefore need to be careful to ensure that the overseas tax position and the position under the Double Tax Treaty was reviewed.

Exemptions from the exit charge?

Certain assets are excluded from the charge. There are two main exemptions from the exit charge:

☐ If the company that is migrating continues to trade in the UK through a branch or agency then, even though it has become non-resident, it will be within the charge to Corporation Tax as regards certain assets.

Assets which are situated in the UK and are used for the purposes of the trade or branch or agency are then exempted from the exit charge. Therefore a company that trades from the UK, and holds UK trading property (eg offices, warehouses, factories etc) would not include any uplift in value on these assets when calculating the exit charge.

☐ Secondly it is possible to defer the charge on foreign assets of a foreign trade where a subsidiary company migrates but the principal company remains resident in the UK. The charge on deemed disposals, may be partly or wholly postponed if the following conditions apply immediately after the relevant time:

o assets are situated outside the UK and are used in or for the purposes of a trade carried on outside the UK (`foreign assets'),

o the chargeable company is a 75 per cent subsidiary of a company which is resident in the UK, the `principal company',

o the chargeable company and the principal company elect for postponement within two years of the relevant time.

This will therefore apply where a UK subsidiary of another UK company transfers residence overseas. Any UK assets used for a UK trade would qualify for the exemption under the above provision. Any foreign assets used for an overseas trade would qualify under this provision.

Against EU law

The EU has looked at exit charges in a number of cases (eg the Lasteyrie case for individuals and more recently the Cartesio case).

In early 2012 the EU issued the UK with a "reasoned opinion" requesting the UK to amend the exit charge provisions.

Following this, the UK has introduced measures providing for qualifying companies migrating from the UK to another EU or EEA member state to elect, temporarily, to defer for up to 10 years the payment of exit charges on gains and profits deemed to arise when a company ceases to be UK resident.

The new measures are effective retrospectively, allowing for elections to defer in respect of accounting periods ended on or after 10 March 2012.

As the measures were prompted by a requirement of EU law, only companies formed in accordance with the laws of an EU or EEA member state and who transfer their tax residence from the UK to another EU or EEA state qualify.

Qualifying companies may enter into an exit charge payment plan with HMRC, agreeing a schedule of payments of tax and interest in accordance with either of two methods:

• the standard installment method: the exit charge is payable in six equal annual installments.

The first installment is due nine months and one day after the end of the last accounting period in which the qualifying company is resident in the UK for tax purposes.

Repayments may, however, be accelerated in a number of scenarios, including insolvency and relocation to a state outside the EU or EEA; and

• the realisation method: the exit charge is payable in annual installments on the basis of how the value of the various assets of the company, subject to the charge, is expected to be realised.

Qualifying companies will be required to provide HMRC with annual reports detailing the realisation of its exit charge assets and liabilities.

In all cases, the maximum number of annual installments is ten, the first of which is due nine months and one day after the end of the last accounting period in which the qualifying company is resident in the UK for tax purposes.

There may be fewer annual installments if the assets and liabilities in question are realised sooner.

Restructuring

The big problem with a transfer of the effective management above is the exit charge on the gains in the company when it leaves the UK.

Given such difficulties, the larger corporate groups look to achieve the benefits of migration by creating an offshore holding company.

They would achieve this by interposing a new non-UK holding company between the UK company and its shareholders. ie the shareholders now own shares in a non resident company, which then owns the UK company.

This is relatively straightforward and can be achieved by a share for share exchange provided the share exchange is accepted as being for bona fide commercial purposes.

If not then you'd be looking at further reorganising to implement the holding company.

You'd need to ensure that the holding company was genuinely managed from abroad to ensure it was not UK resident and was exempt from UK corporation tax on overseas income.

The key advantage in having an offshore holding company is that:

(1) it can receive overseas income streams generally free of UK tax, and

(2) it can hold shares in CFC's without being subject to the onerous CFC provisions.

The exit charge is avoided as the UK company would still be controlled from the UK, but the shareholders can obtain the benefits of the tax treatment offshore company.

It used to be advisable to implement 'income access' arrangements to allow shareholders to extract dividends from the UK company.

However, now that the tax credit has been extended to UK residents on overseas dividends, for most UK shareholders this would not be necessary, and they could extract cash directly from the offshore company.

CHAPTER 17
USING A UK COMPANY IN OFFSHORE TAX PLANNING

For many non residents, UK entities and other tax planning vehicles have become of increasing importance when looking at structuring their overseas investments.

This is in part due to the fact that the UK doesn't appear on any blacklists and therefore will as a rule attract less attention from overseas tax authorities than other blacklisted countries.

The UK can be used as a stepping stone in a number of ways:

Treaty non resident

Although a UK incorporated company is typically subject to UK corporation tax at 20% it can gain significant advantages if it's treaty resident overseas.

Under the provisions a company incorporated in the UK, but qualifying as a resident of some other country for the purposes of a tax treaty, is to be treated for UK tax purposes as not UK resident.

This is clearly very attractive in terms of UK tax, as a non resident company would be exempt from UK tax on gains as well as overseas income.

In terms of overseas tax you'd need to ensure that the treaty was with a country that taxed the company profits at low or nil rates eg:

☐ A company incorporated in the UK but resident in Mauritius may have a tax rate as low as 1.5%.

☐ A company resident in Singapore will pay no tax on any of its foreign income,

☐ A company resident in Malaysia will be exempt from tax on most foreign income

☐ A company resident in Barbados will pay local tax on its foreign income only if it remits income to Barbados. None of these countries levy any tax on capital gains.

Therefore a UK incorporated company treaty resident in a suitable jurisdiction can have the best of both worlds.

UK holding company

A UK company can be very attractive as a holding company. For example there could be an operating company, resident in a high-tax country, which is owned by an investor in a zero-tax jurisdiction.

By interposing a UK holding company, dividends may be free of withholding tax, or suffer a lower rate of withholding tax than would be suffered if the dividends were paid direct to the investor.

This is because the UK holding company can benefit from a tax treaty or from EU the Parent/Subsidiary Directive.

The UK though has another benefit as it doesn't levy any tax on outgoing dividends. Therefore the shareholders resident abroad don't need to worry about rerouting dividends or other tax planning strategies to reduce withholding taxes.

Corporate Partner

Another way of using a UK company is as the managing partner in a limited liability partnership. Partnerships are transparent for tax purposes.

Therefore where a partner is non-resident and the partnership income has a non-UK source, the partner has no UK tax liability.

Typically, the UK company will be a form of nominee and be entitled to only a small share of the profits under the profit sharing agreements. Most of the income will go to the overseas partners.

Customers, will however, deal with the UK partner, and may by so doing be able to circumvent blacklist and other problems.

Note that unlike a company the tax liability is not usually affected by the "management and control" of the business.

Therefore if the partners want to have partnership meetings in London and take decisions there about the management and control of the partnership business, they can do so. They would though need to ensure that there was no UK trade (otherwise the profits would be subject to UK tax).

CHAPTER 18
USING AN OFFSHORE SUBSIDIARY TO AVOID UK CORPORATION TAX

Companies looking to expand overseas could use an offshore company to potentially avoid UK corporation tax.

The company would still need to be non resident in order to avoid UK corporation tax on the foreign trade.

Therefore it would need to have foreign directors actually operating the company at a senior level. The UK parent company would therefore need to ensure that the foreign directors actually exercised real control over the company and that they didn't just rubber stamp decisions of the UK parent company.

However, if the foreign subsidiary was non resident the profits from the overseas trade could potentially accumulate free of UK corporation tax in the offshore company providing the CFC rules are avoided.

Note that an offshore subsidiary is only an effective shelter if a taxable presence in high tax jurisdictions is avoided. The rules as to the extent of a taxable presence vary from country to country and therefore local advice should be taken in the countries trades will be carried out.

What are the "CFC" Rules?

I mentioned above that a non resident subsidiary can be attractive providing the CFC rules are avoided.

The CFC rules are therefore very important for any company that wants to set up an overseas subsidiary.

If the CFC rules apply, the UK company will have to pay tax on the overseas company's profits, provided the percentage of profits apportioned is at least 25%.

You should note that the UK CFC regime will not apply if you are an individual owning an overseas company.

Before falling within the CFC rules a company would firstly need to meet the definition of a 'controlled foreign company'.

A controlled foreign company (CFC) is one which is resident outside the UK, controlled by persons resident in the UK.

'Control' is determined by considering the rights of the UK residents with an interest in the company, together with any rights held by persons connected with the UK resident.

Broadly, a person will have control if they have power to secure that the affairs of the company are conducted in accordance with their wishes, where that power arises through shareholdings, voting power, or by the documents governing the non-UK company.

So although the foreign subsidiary may have an overseas board of directors exercising control (to make it non resident for UK tax purposes), given it's a subsidiary of a UK company it would fall within the CFC rules.

Purpose of the CFC Rules

The CFC regime attempts to prevent UK companies from artificially diverting profits away from the UK and into low tax jurisdictions.

Such diversion is more likely to occur in businesses where income is mobile, such as royalties, interest, consultancy fees, or where the overseas entity has large trade related connections with UK customers or suppliers.

Effectively the taxpayer is presumed 'guilty' unless it could get itself into one of the prescribed exemptions.

If the overseas subsidiary is deemed to be a CFC its profits are added to those of the UK company and subject to UK corporation tax.

New CFC Rules

The new rules, which are essentially anti-avoidance rules designed to prevent a company from artificially moving its profits abroad to a country with more favourable tax rates, came into effect for accounting periods beginning on or after 1 January 2013.

Where the CFC rules apply some or all of the CFC's profits will be allocated to the UK company that controls it and the UK company will be taxed on this amount.

Exemption from CFC Rules

Certain types of company and income are exempt from the CFC rules.

- Entity Level Exemptions - these are a series of exemptions. Where a CFC qualifies under one of these exemptions the entire income of the CFC will be outside the scope of the CFC rules, and the group need not concern itself with the CFC provisions in relation to this company.

- Gateway Provisions - these examine the activities of the CFC and essentially leave only those profits which have been artificially diverted from the UK, those within the gateway, under the scope of the CFC rules and hence taxable in the UK.

Entity Level Exemptions

The following are full entity level exemptions:

- Exempt period exemption -- This exemption applies for the first 12 months after a non-resident company comes under UK control. There will be no CFC charge providing any necessary restructuring is undertaken to ensure that no CFC charges arise in subsequent periods.

- Excluded territories exemption -- CFCs resident in specific territories, broadly those with a headline tax rate of more than 75% of the UK tax rate, will be exempt, provided that their total income within certain categories does not exceed 10% of the company's pre-tax profits for the accounting period, or £50,000 if greater. This exemption will not be available where significant IP has been transferred to the CFC from the UK during the accounting period or the previous six years.

- Low profits exemption -- A CFC will be exempt if its accounting profits do not exceed £50,000 in an accounting period, or if its accounting profits do not exceed £500,000 and its non-trading income does not exceed £50,000.

- Low profit margin exemption -- A CFC will be exempt provided its accounting profits do not exceed 10% of relevant operating expenditure.

- Low level of tax exemption -- A CFC that has paid local tax of at least 75% of the amount it would have paid as a UK resident company, will be exempt.

Gateway Provisions

Should the entity level provisions above not apply, then the gateway provisions need to be considered to determine if profit passes through the CFC gateways and therefore should be subject to UK taxation.

There are a number of gateways specified in the various chapters of the legislation and for each gateway it is necessary to establish whether the applicable test applies, and, if so, which profits pass through the gateway.

The CFC charge gateway tests are as follows:
- Chapter 4: Profits attributable to UK activities
- Chapter 5: Non-trading finance profits

- Chapter 6: Trading finance profits
- Chapter 7: Captive insurance business
- Chapter 8: Solo consideration

Chapter 4 - Profits Attributable to UK Activities

Chapter 4 will apply if the CFC has business profits (other than property business profits and non-trading finance profits), in circumstances where the CFC is unable to satisfy at least one of the following tests:

- the CFC does not hold assets or risks under an arrangement to avoid tax;
- the CFC does not have any UK managed assets or bear any UK controlled risks; and
- the CFC could operate effectively if its UK managed assets or UK controlled risks were managed/controlled other than from the UK.

Chapter 4 includes a number of exclusions which prevent a CFC's profits passing through the gateway, for example; where those profits arise mainly from non-UK activities or where they relate to arrangements entered into with group companies where those arrangements could have been entered into with independent enterprises.

Chapters 5 to 8 Gateway Tests

Chapters 5, 6, 7 and 8 gateway tests are specifically designed for CFCs with certain non trading finance profits, trading finance profits, insurance companies and CFCs consolidated with regulated UK financial companies. Unless the CFC falls into these categories, it will only be the Chapter 4 gateway that will need to be considered.

Chapter 5 - Non-Trading Finance Profits

Non-trading finance profits, which are incidental to business profits, will not pass through the gateway. Full or partial (75%) exemption may apply with regard to non-trading finance profits from qualifying loan relationships.

Chapter 6 - Trading Finance Profits

Only trading finance profits which derive from UK connected capital contributions will pass through the gateway. The profits of a group treasury company are treated as non-trading finance profits and therefore do not fall within this category. This enables such companies to access the full or partial (75%) finance company exemptions.

Chapter 7 - Captive Insurance Business

Profits from captive insurance business will pass through the gateway where the contract of insurance is entered into with:

- a UK resident person connected with the CFC; or
- a non-UK resident person connected with the CFC acting through a UK permanent establishment; or
- a UK resident person where the contract is linked with the provision of services or goods to the UK resident person.

Chapter 8 - Solo Consideration

Applies where the CFC is controlled by a UK resident bank.

Summary

It is important that the new CFC rules are clearly understood by all non-UK resident companies controlled by persons in the UK. Due to the exemptions and the various gateways there may be legitimate opportunities to reduce the UK tax payable.

CHAPTER 19
STRUCTURING YOUR BUSINESS OR COMPANY PRIOR TO A DISPOSAL

When looking to reduce tax on the sale of your business or company, the first aspect to consider is the form of business entity, and exactly what is to be sold. The form of business entity would usually be considered at the date of start up, and the essential distinction is between a UK company, offshore company, trading personally or via a partnership.

Using a company has advantages in that not only does it provide for a measure of protection for the traders personal assets (house, investments etc) but it can also reduce the ongoing tax liabilities on the business profits, where some of the business profits are reinvested in the business.

As many businesses will not look to extract significant sums for a number of years, using a company could reduce the tax rate to 20%, from 40% or 45%.

In addition, there could be a saving in national insurance, as the company would not be subject to NIC on profits arising, but a sole trader or partner would.

However on disposal, unless you can structure a disposal as a disposal of the shares, there could be a nasty CGT shock.

When using a company you have two options for the disposal. You could sell the shares or alternatively the company could sell the assets. If you traded personally you would simply sell the assets/trade directly.

Generally speaking for most UK residents a disposal personally will be much more attractive than a company disposal due to Entrepreneurs Relief.

A disposal of business assets (which included shares in your personal trading companies as well as an interest in a business) reduce the CGT rate to 10% after one year. This is a massive tax benefit and usually a company disposal could not compete.

If the company did sell the assets not only would it not be entitled to claim Entrepreneurs relief, but you'd then also need to consider extracting the cash from company. Fine if you are an expat as you can just take a dividend free of UK income tax (subject to the temporary non residence provisions), but if you're UK resident you will be subject to a further 25% (or 30.55% if above £150,000) income tax charge for all amounts in excess of the basic rate tax band.

Therefore if you do own a company the best option is usually to sell the shares in the company. The gain will then arise on you, and you can look at claiming Entrepreneurs Relief.

This though depends on whether the purchaser wants to buy the shares. A problem particularly with property type businesses is that a purchaser may well see the company's assets as a short term resale opportunity.

Therefore if they acquire the shares they will be 'inheriting' the previous tax liability, as any gain since the company originally acquired the property(s) will come into charge when the property's are sold.

In this case, although the purchaser may well agree to a share purchase, you'll usually find that a discount is made for the company's tax liability up to the date of the share disposal. This will eliminate any tax benefits to you of the share disposal route.

This should really be considered at the original start up, as if in this case the business was owned personally the tax savings could be substantial due to the enhanced reliefs.

Therefore choosing the type of entity would not usually be undertaken immediately prior to a disposal unless you are carrying on a business as a sole trader and and want to arrange for a disposal of shares in a company, rather than a direct disposal of assets.

The main reason for this would be if you run a UK business but are also looking to emigrate from the UK personally.

In this case there are some big advantages to transferring the business to a company before you leave the UK.

The reason for this is that although as a non UK resident you are exempt from UK CGT on gains, this does not apply to gains arising from a UK branch or agency trade (ie where there is a permanent establishment).

Therefore if you are carrying out a trade from the UK even if you leave the UK you could find yourself subject to UK CGT.

A simple way around this is to incorporate the business before you leave the UK. There are some tax reliefs that allow a trading business to transfer all of its assets to a company without a tax charge. You could then leave the UK and sell the shares in the company free of UK CGT as a non UK resident.

I mentioned above that an overseas company could be used as one of the types of entities. In most cases UK resident and domiciled individuals would achieve no tax benefit by using an offshore company.

If you were planning to leave the UK or if you had overseas partners/directors the position would be completely different but unless these apply, for MOST UK residents they would find obtaining tax benefits from an offshore structure difficult.

Other assets

A big problem with a company is that if you want to sell the shares in the company (which as we've seen above will minimise tax for many UK residents) you can't pick and choose which parts of the business are to be sold.

If you own the business personally or the company is selling the assets you could select which assets are to be sold and which ones retained.

When you sell the shares these relate to shares in the whole company, and therefore the whole of the business/assets, and therefore ensuring that the company contains the parts of the business and other assets that you want to sell is very important.

This is often a problem with a company that has been used to undertake two trades or where an investment property is held in a trading company.

You would then need to extract the trade that you wished to retain/property.

A simple transfer of a trade or the property out of the company should be avoided as this would not only be a taxable chargeable gain but unless full consideration was payable to the company for the transfer an income tax charge could arise on the shareholders.

There are basically two ways to achieve the transfer of assets out of the company tax efficiently.

Hive Up

This would work by the shareholder using the share for share exchange provisions to form a new holding company and the property could be transferred out of the company free of tax.

Example

Giles owned all of the shares in Giles UK Ltd which owned a commercial property and a trading business. He could form a new company (Giles Investments) which would acquire the shares in Giles UK Ltd from Giles in return for an issue of shares by Giles Investments to Giles.

The position would then be that Giles would own the shares in Giles Investments.

The property could then be transferred free of any immediate tax charge to Giles Investments.

This would be good as Giles UK Ltd would then hold just the trading business and would be a much more attractive option for a trade purchaser.

Demerger

Essentially this can be used to split a company either where there are two trades being carried on, or where there is a trade and an investment business.

Broadly there are two methods of carrying out a demerger.

The first utilises a specific legislation introduced for this purpose and the second used the insolvency legislation.

Under either case you could use these provisions to transfer assets or trades out of the company to ensure that you are selling only the assets you want to sell (and the assets that the purchaser wants to buy).

Excess cash and pre sale dividend

If the company has a large cash balance, and if Entrepreneurs Relief is not due a tax efficient option is often to extract cash from the company as a dividend.

The effective tax rate on this will be likely to be 25% if within the higher rate band, but the CGT rate if the shares had been owned would be in the region of 28%. In this case it would then make sense to extract the cash before the disposal by way of a dividend.

Clearly if you'd qualify for Entrepreneurs Relief on the shares this would be less attractive. Having said that Entrepreneurs Relief is only given to trading companies.

The Revenue will refuse to treat a company with substantial non trading assets as a trading company, and therefore if there was a large cash balance in the company, this could in itself prevent business asset status.

It would then be important to consider whether the extraction of cash as a dividend could revive business asset status a couple of years before a disposal to maximise relief.

Previous liabilities

One of big problems with a share disposal is that from the purchasers perspective it is the most 'risky'. They won't just be acquiring a bundle of assets and liabilities like they would under an asset deal. As the company has a separate legal entity they'll also be taking on any company liabilities.

Therefore from the purchasers perspective the risk is that they'll be sued for something that happened before they even owned the shares.

In order to protect the purchaser the disposal contract will be every comprehensive and include a raft of warranties and indemnities for you to sign to try and protect the purchaser as much as possible.

If this doesn't sound appealing you could look to a hive down to meet your and the purchasers requirements.

A hive down is essentially a cross between an asset purchase and a share deal.

The seller company would transfer its trade and assets to a new company, and this new company is then acquired by the purchaser.

It's of benefit to purchasers as it allows a share purchase but also allows them to acquire a company holding those assets and the part of the business which the seller wants to dispose of, and which the purchaser wishes to acquire.

This means that it allows the purchaser to acquire a 'clean' company which does not come with any bad history and with no risk of any skeletons jumping out of the closet.

There are some special tax reliefs which can be available using the hive down route to ensure that the transfer can be made free of tax however the main tax advantage to the purchaser would be the ability to transfer any losses to the new company.

What you'll be looking to achieve is to put together a package that fits in with both you and your purchasers requirements. This could therefore include removing any surplus assets, using a newco to arrange a share disposal or arranging a hive down to provide a clean company.

This could even include a straightforward asset disposal by the company for example if:

☐ You were non UK resident and could extract cash from the company free of tax (subject to the new "temporary non resident" provisions from April 2013)

☐ The company had large capital losses to offset any gains

☐ The company would be reinvesting proceeds in other business assets and could make a rollover relief claim (this would not be available if you personally made the reinvestment, but the gain arose to the company).

CHAPTER 20
QUALIFYING FOR ENTREPRENEURS RELIEF WHEN YOUR COMPANY HAS LARGE CASH BALANCES

On a sale of shares you'll only qualify for Entrepreneurs Relief if the company is an unquoted trading company (or the holding company of a trading group).

It is therefore very important to determine whether a company is a trading company, as this can make the difference between receiving or being denied Entrepreneurs Relief.

How Does the Taxman Define a Trading Company?

As you'd expect, there is no simple answer to this question, as each case is approached differently. The tax legislation doesn't include much of a definition of a trading company, so it's simply down to Revenue and Customs and the courts to establish some guidelines.

Thankfully, because of the significant impact that this distinction can have, Revenue has given us some general rules that can be used as a guide.

The legislation on the new Entrepreneurs Relief states that it will follow the old taper relief definition of a trading company.

This states that a company is classed as a trading company provided its activities "... do not include to a substantial extent activities other than trading activities".

Pretty straightforward, and provided a company doesn't have "substantial" non-trading activities there should be no problem qualifying for the relief.

However, the taxman's view of 'substantial' is probably not the same as yours and they would take this to mean more than 20% of the income or assets.

The guidance they've published on this states that they will look at a number of factors including:

• Any income from non-trading activities

• Any non-trading assets held on the balance sheet

• Time spent by directors or employees in non-trading activities

So when looking at whether your company is a trading company, it's probably advisable to review the statutory accounts for the previous six years or so, looking at these measures for any indications of non-trading activities.

The kind of things Revenue and Customs could regard as non-trading include:

• Holding investment property via a company

• Holding shares in other companies (if your company isn't a holding company)

• Having surplus cash on the balance sheet not required for business purposes.

The surplus cash issue is a particularly nasty one, and although it's aimed at so-called 'money box' companies where cash is rolled up in a company, it can apply to genuine trading companies that happen to build up large cash reserves.

How to Get Classed as a Trading Company

The definition of trading company for Entrepreneurs Relief purposes is found in TCGA 1992 s165A(3) which states that "a company carrying on trading activities whose activities do not include to a substantial extent activities other than trading activities".

HMRC interpret substantial as more than 20% and looks at the activities of the company as a whole.

The definition does refer to activities, not assets. In many cases the company is a trading company with large cash balances which has trading turnover well in excess of 80% of the total turnover and well over 80% of employee and management time is devoted to trading activities.

It is only the non trading assets that exceed 20%.

Therefore the argument would be that there is a genuine trading activity even taking account of the surplus cash.

If the cash was actively managed by you it could be argued that this was a non-trading activity, however this is frequently not the case. The only activity is the trading activity.

As I understand it HMRC takes a rounded view of the different activities and transactions undertaken by the company and providing there is a genuine trading activity there should be a good case that the company should qualify for Entrepreneurs Relief.

However, if you wanted to be certain of the position you would either need to consider other options such as extract the cash (at least 12 months before the disposal) or arguing that the cash was required for the future purpose of the business.

When looking at the accounts for the period in question, if you do find there are substantial non-trading activities, you'll then need to consider whether these can be satisfactorily explained to the tax inspector so that they don't 'taint' the status of the company. The two main exemptions from the non-trading rules are:

• Time period.

When looking at the status of the company you would usually examine the position over the course of a number of financial years.

It may well be the case that in some years the 20% threshold was exceeded, and in others it wasn't. In this case it could be in your interests to take an average position over the entire period.

In such cases HMRC have been known to accept that, although in one or two isolated years non-trading income had been substantial, when compared with total receipts over the entire period in question the 20% threshold was not breached.

• Reasonably required for business purposes.

The other main option is to argue that although the 20% threshold has been breached, this does not amount to a non-trading activity.

This would mainly apply to cash held on the balance sheet, particularly where the cash is invested.

For the cash to amount to a non-trading activity it would need to be shown that it was not reasonably required for business purposes.

Therefore retaining the cash to avoid incurring a personal tax charge on extraction would not be a good enough reason to avoid being classed as a non-trading purpose.

If you did manage to establish that the cash was used for a business purpose, then it's unlikely that HMRC would restrict trading status.

To do this you'll need to look at the specific business environment and requirements of your particular trade. It may be, for example, that you were required to retain a fixed level of cash on deposit (as in the case of bookmakers, insurance agencies and travel agencies), which would clearly be a persuasive argument that you held the cash for a business purpose.

Any legal duty or recommendation from a trade association, for example, for a certain level of liquid assets would be likely to satisfy the taxman.

Similarly if your company had sold a part of its operations and was holding the proceeds on deposit while seeking out potential acquisitions, this would also be likely to be accepted as a trading purpose. Any future business purpose could be acceptable.

CHAPTER 21
QUALIFYING FOR INHERITANCE TAX RELIEF WHEN YOUR COMPANY HAS LARGE CASH BALANCES

Any shares that you own would be included in your estate and potentially subject to 40% Inheritance Tax (IHT).

However if the company is an unquoted trading company you should consider whether business property relief would apply. This can provide for a 100% exemption from inheritance tax.

Where an unquoted trading company holds an amount of cash which is in excess of the amount which is needs for its business, it is likely that the cash will be treated as an excepted asset and excluded from business property relief.

This is because under IHTA84/S112 (1) the value of any "excepted assets" is to be left out of account for the purposes of business relief. In order not to be "excepted" an asset must pass one of two tests:

• It must have been used wholly or mainly for the purposes of the business in question throughout the two years, immediately preceding the gift or date of death

• Alternatively it must be required at the time of the transfer of value for future use for the purposes of the business in question.

If the cash is surplus to requirements then it could be viewed as an excepted asset with the result that the amount of BPR on the shares would be restricted.

If however there was a sound commercial reason for the build up of cash you could argue that it did not constitute an excepted asset.
It has been pointed out to HMRC recently that in the current economic climate many businesses are retaining increased cash reserves to protect themselves against any further downtown in trade.

However, HMRC are not impressed. They say that to avoid treatment as an excepted asset there needs to be evidence that the cash is held for an identifiable future purpose.

This may in fact be overstating the position. Section 112 only requires the cash to be required for the future use for the purposes of the business. There may therefore be a number of things in contemplation.

HMRC consider that the holding of funds as a buffer to weather the economic climate is not sufficient reason to prevent it being an excepted asset.

What to do?

HMRC may be viewing the position unsympathetically but the taxpayer is able to protect himself .

The problem is that the holding of cash on deposit is not generally regarded as an investment business by reason of the decision in Barclays Bank Trust Co v CIR.

It therefore represents an excepted asset if it is not required for the future use in the business.

However, if this surplus cash were to be invested otherwise than on pure cash deposit, then it would become an investment business and providing this investment business was not more important than the overall trading business, then it would not be an excepted asset and no problem would arise. The company would still be wholly or mainly a trading company and the existence of the subservient investment business would not interfere with the business property relief.

CHAPTER 22
TAX PLANNING FOR NON UK RESIDENTS OWNING UK PROPERTY

It's often the case that individuals own UK properties via a UK company.

When any such individuals move overseas and lose UK residence they will usually still hold the UK properties via the company.

The company has a liability to UK corporation tax on any rental profits. The shareholder can extract the remaining profits free of UK income tax/withholding tax and could always sell the shares in the company free of capital gains tax. Any disposal by the company though would be subject to corporation tax on any uplift in value of the properties.

One issue that is often of key importance is in relation to funding the properties.

The financing in the company could come either from the UK or overseas.

UK financing is often preferred. The reason for this is that the UK company would obtain a corporation tax deduction for the interest, and any funds held offshore by the shareholder would be free of income tax.

If financing is obtained from overseas the risk is that the tax deduction at source rules could apply. These can require tax to be deducted by the payer where the interest is from a UK source but the payment is made overseas.

The key issue is where the 'source' of the interest is. Revenue and Customs would look at a number of factors to determine whether the interest has a UK source:

- The residence of the debtor (this is usually taken to be the place where the debt will be enforced),

- The source from which interest is paid,

- Where the interest is paid, and

- The nature and location of any security for the debt.

If the loan was made to a UK company from overseas and in respect of UK property it would be likely that the interest would have a UK source and as such be subject to the deduction of tax at source rules. Therefore whilst it would be deductible for the UK company when calculating it's taxable profits there could be a 20% income tax liability on the interest.

The options to avoid this are limited if the interest is paid overseas. A payment to a UK bank avoids these issues.

The main option to reduce withholding tax on interest paid overseas would be to rely on a double tax treaty. These provide for an exemption or reduction in UK tax deducted at source depending on the particular agreement that the UK has with the country in question. You could therefore ensure that the deduction at source from the UK was eliminated.

Transferring properties to an offshore company?

Another option would be to transfer the properties to an offshore company. The initial consideration here would be any capital gains tax on the transfer to an offshore company. Your best bet here would be if there had been only a nominal increase in value.

A transfer overseas would be advantageous in terms of any future capital gains on a disposal of the properties.

If held via a UK company any increase in value would be subject to UK corporation tax on the gains (ie 20%).

If held by a non resident UK tax on the gain could be avoided if the properties were commercial properties (residential property is subject to CGT for all non-residents from April 2015). The rental income would then be within the non resident landlord scheme and an application would need to be made to receive the interest gross (without UK income tax deducted on the rental income).

Income tax (note not corporation tax) would be assessed via a self assessment return. Any interest paid to a non resident lender could still be claimed as a tax deduction in calculating the UK taxable profits. However the tax deduction of source provisions apply where interest is paid overseas and has a UK source.

Therefore it could still apply to a non resident paying interest overseas although it would provide you with a stronger argument that the interest had a non UK source.

Another benefit of holding the properties via a non UK company would be if the shareholder had lost UK domicile. A non UK domiciliary would be subject to UK inheritance tax on the value of the UK shares if it was not a trading company. By contrast a non domiciliary wouldn't be subject to inheritance tax on the value of overseas shares if the UK properties were held via an offshore company.

CHAPTER 23
USING A DIRECTORS LOAN ACCOUNT TO REDUCE TAX

A directors loan account can be very attractive in reducing UK tax.

Essentially it applies where the company owes you money. It's shown as a creditor in the accounts and you can extract funds from this as and when you choose free of income tax and national insurance.

Where you owe the company money there are some nasty avoidance rules which can mean that the company has to pay a 25% tax charge and you are also subject to tax on the interest free or low interest element.

These provisions though don't apply where the loan is from you to the company. You can therefore make the loan interest free or have it as a full commercial interest bearing loan. Whatever the position the loan repayments are still free of tax for you.

Note though if it's an interest bearing loan the interest element will be treated separately. The interest would be allowed as a tax deduction under the loan relationship provisions (effectively giving you a corporation tax deduction). However it would then be subject to income tax in your hands.

When will a directors loan account arise?

It will occur whenever you transfer any asset undertake services for the company and do not receive full consideration.

If you therefore transferred a car to the company which was valued at £5,000, you may not take any funds from the company to represent the £5,000 value. In this case you could either show this as a debt from the company or simply as a form of capital contribution by you.

Therefore the company would hold an asset at £5,000 and would either show a credit to loan account of £5,000 or a capital credit to the shareholders funds of £5,000. If a debt is established it allows the repayment to be made in the future free of tax.

It's for this reason that in many cases a sale -- rather than a gift may be preferred. What you will have to beware of though is:

- Stamp duty. If you sell rather than gift land or property to the company there is likely to be a stamp duty charge. By contrast a simple gift to a company may well not attract any stamp duty as there's no 'chargeable consideration'.

- Gift relief. If you gift business assets you can often claim gift relief to defer any capital gain arising on the transfer. However gift relief is restricted or even eliminated where some proceeds are received.

You therefore need to be very careful when deciding whether to sell for full consideration or to gift for nil consideration.

One of the key occasions when a directors loan account often arises is on the incorporation of a business. This simply means that the business is transferred to a company.

In this case, the business owner could sell the business to the company for full market value. They'd pay capital gains tax on the transfer at 18%/28% or 10% if Entrepreneurs Relief was available.

The proceeds could be left outstanding if it did not have the immediate funds and the shareholders/directors could then extract free of income tax as and when they chose. They'd therefore potentially suffer an immediate 10% CGT charge but save income tax at 40 (or 45% if they were additional rate taxpayers).

If they didn't want to suffer any CGT charge on the transfer they could claim gift relief. However by gifting the business no loan account would be established. Often business owners will gift part of the business and sell the remainder a full value.

Use could always be made of the annual exemption. So for instance an asset valued at £100K but with a £20K gain could be put into joint names of a husband and wife and transferred to the company. The gain would be offset by the annual CGT exemptions and the £100K could then be extracted free of tax.

Any transfer of assets to a company should therefore always be considered in terms of the potential impact on the loan account. If you can also arrange for a tax free transfer into the company you've achieved a 'double whammy' in tax terms as it'll be completely free of tax.

CHAPTER 24
NEW CAPITAL ALLOWANCE RULES FROM APRIL 2014

Businesses can claim capital allowances as a deduction from their tax calculation on the expenditure they have incurred on fixtures in a building, including for example hot and cold water systems, air conditioning, heating systems and lifts.

Capital allowances are claimed over a number of years as a percentage of the expenditure on a reducing basis. Where a building is sold then the buyer can claim capital allowances on the part of the price that relates to fixtures, so long as the buyer is carrying on a qualifying activity for capital allowances purposes.

Prior to April 2012 where a building contained fixtures, the parties could fix the part of the price apportioned to the fixtures by agreeing what is known as a section 198 election. Alternatively if no apportionment was agreed, the buyer could make its own apportionment on a just and reasonable basis.

Now the rules are more restrictive. The buyer of a secondhand building will only be able to make a claim for capital allowances if it can show that two new requirements are met. These are:

- The pooling requirement
- The fixed value requirement

This April sees the commencement of the two major changes to the capital allowances regime, introduced by the Finance Act 2012 and referred to as the "pooling requirement" and the "fixed value requirement".

The purpose of these changes is to address HMRC's concern that buyers were claiming excessive capital allowances and HMRC could do nothing about it as they did not have sufficient records to ascertain the correct level of allowances. The new rules require owners to "pool" their qualifying expenditure on fixtures in a tax return (thus bringing the expenditure into the capital allowances system at an early date) and "fix" the value of the fixtures on a sale (thus providing a "road map" of disposal and acquisition values made by successive owners).

Pooling

Owners will need to allocate their expenditure on fixtures to a pool in a chargeable period beginning before the owner sells the fixtures. Even if a seller has not pooled its expenditure on fixtures at the time it sells the fixtures, it could nevertheless satisfy the pooling requirement by including it in its tax return for the chargeable period in which the sale takes place or (subject to complying with the applicable time limits) by amending a return, for an earlier chargeable period. "Pooling" the expenditure does not mean that the owner has to claim the allowances.

All it means is that the owner has to include a computation of the expenditure in a tax return.

This will enable the owner to transfer the allowances (and get value for them) on a sale of the property. An owner should pool its expenditure on fixtures even when it is a person that is not entitled to claim allowances (for example, a pension fund), in order to be able to transfer the allowances on a sale of the property.

Failure to meet this requirement means that the buyer (and the buyer's successors) will not be able to claim allowances in respect of those fixtures. This means that any unclaimed capital allowances will be lost unless action is taken to pool the allowances (at the latest) when a sale of the property takes place.

The fixed value requirement

On a sale of a property that includes fixtures, the seller and the buyer will also have to satisfy the fixed value requirement in order to pass on any capital allowances and can do so in one of the following ways:

- the seller and the buyer join in a section 198 election (or, in the case of the grant of a lease, a section 199 election); or

- the First-tier Tribunal, on an application by the seller or the buyer, determine the amount of the price that should be apportioned to the fixtures (this will be done on the just and reasonable basis).

The fixed value requirement must be satisfied within two years of the date that the buyer acquired the fixtures (and the property).

In most cases this will be met by having a section 198 (or 199) election.

What do the new rules mean?

- Capital allowances provisions in sale agreements will have to be detailed and they are more likely, therefore, to be more heavily negotiated as a result of the new rules.

- A seller will need to ensure that it has carried out a detailed review of its capital allowances history and is able to make available to a buyer all relevant tax returns and computations.

- A buyer is likely to ask more detailed questions on the capital allowances history and will want comfort in the sale agreement that the seller has (or will) meet the pooling requirement.

- The fixed value requirement means that, most of the time, a section 198 election will be required and, therefore, this will be provided for in the sale agreement. The amount to be included in the election will need to be considered carefully by the seller and agreed with the buyer.

CHAPTER 25
NEW PROPOSALS FOR DISCLOSURE OF BENEFICIAL OWNERS

Major beneficial owners of UK companies (and limited liability partnerships) will have to be identified and their names, nationality and addresses publicly disclosed, the Government has decided.

In other measures designed to enhance transparency and trust in UK companies, corporate directors will be largely prohibited and bearer shares will be phased out. And to make it easier to obtain redress from those who exercise influence or control over a company via a "front" or stooge director, the Companies Act is likely to be amended to specify that a person who controls a director will be treated as a shadow director, and that shadow directors are subject to directors' general statutory duties.

Disclosure of beneficial owners

Companies will have a continuing obligation to identify and record who their beneficial owners are. To enable them to do so, new powers will be introduced that are expected to be similar to those currently used by public companies to investigate which persons are "interested" in their shares (using so-called section 793 notices).

Beneficial owners will also have a continuing obligation to disclose their identity and certain details to the company, including how their beneficial interest is held. A central registry of company beneficial ownership information will be created and maintained by Companies House.

Members of the public will be able to inspect both the register kept by Companies House and that kept by the relevant company, subject to certain exceptions: for example, as with the existing rules relating to directors' details, a person's residential address will not be open to public inspection, and a person at serious risk of violence or intimidation will be able to apply for his details to be kept from the public.

The Government is considering further how far members of the public should be able to see information that would normally be kept confidential for legitimate commercial reasons -- such as the details of trust arrangements, limited liability partnership agreements and shareholder agreements.

To be incorporated, the founders of a company will have to provide an initial statement of beneficial ownership, and the company will have to confirm that this information is correct at least once every 12 months, or provide details of any changes.

A beneficial owner for this purpose will be a person who "ultimately" owns or controls 25% of a company's shares or voting rights or who "otherwise exercises control" over the management of the company: this is the same test as is used in "know your client" checks done by banks.

To prevent the unscrupulous avoiding the disclosure requirements by splitting a 25% holding up among their family and friends, the holdings of associates will have be aggregated. Where a qualifying beneficial interest is held through a trust, the trustees and any other natural persons who exercise control over the trust will need to be disclosed and registered.

The requirement to obtain, hold and file beneficial ownership information at Companies House will apply to UK bodies corporate that currently file information on their members at Companies House. Companies limited by guarantee and limited liability partnerships will be subject to similar requirements.

Non-UK companies will not be subject to the new rules, but the Government will continue to lobby other jurisdictions, especially via the G8, G20 and EU, to introduce similar rules requiring the disclosure of beneficial owners.

Corporate directors

Unlike Germany, Australia and some other countries, UK law currently permits the use of corporate directors.

According to the Government, "this can result in a lack of transparency and accountability with respect to the individuals influencing the company".

The Government is therefore persuaded that corporate directors should generally be banned. However, it recognises that in some circumstances their use can be legitimate and proper: it therefore proposes to allow corporate directors to be used in "group structures including large listed companies… and large private companies", in charities and OEICs, and as corporate trustees, although it is going to consider such circumstances further.

Bearer shares

It will no longer be possible to create new bearer shares, and companies will be given a period of time -- likely to be nine months from the date when the new legislation receives Royal Assent - to convert existing bearer shares to ordinary registered shares.

After the specified period, companies with bearer shares remaining will have to apply to court for an order cancelling the shares. Bearer shares (technically known as share warrants to bearer) are shares the legal title to which is evidenced by possession of a certificate, rather than entry of the owner's name in the company's register of members.

Ownership of bearer shares can therefore be transferred simply by delivering the certificate to another person, without the company being involved or knowing of the transfer. It is unusual for a UK company to issue bearer shares, but they are more common in some other jurisdictions.

CHAPTER 26
THE PATENT BOX AND THE 10% RATE OF

CORPORATION TAX

As from 1 April 2013 the new Patent Box has been introduced.

This is a new tax regime for Intellectual Property ("IP") that reduces the corporation tax rate payable by UK companies on profits from qualifying IP.

The Patent Box is part of a package of tax changes intended by the UK Government to encourage multinationals to base their operations, in particular tech and innovation activities in the UK.

Other countries such as the Netherlands, Luxembourg, Ireland or Switzerland have advantageous IP regimes and this will allow the UK to compete with these jurisdictions.

What is the Patent Box?

The Patent Box effectively applies a reduced UK corporation tax rate of 10% (the main rate now being 20%) to profits arising from 'qualifying IP rights' that are 'actively owned'.

What IP qualifies for the Box?

Qualifying IP rights are broadly registered patents granted by the UK or European patent office, as well as certain other similar rights such as data exclusivity and plant variety rights.

It is also intended that the regime will apply to national patents of other EU member states to the extent such states have similar patent criteria as the UK.

Such patents can either be owned directly or by way of an exclusive license to exploit such patents in a designated national territory.

Importantly, for a patent to qualify, the company (or a member of the same group as the company) must have made a significant contribution to the development of the patent or an item that incorporates such patent. The Box will not apply to income derived from pre-developed patents that are acquired and then merely exploited.

Active ownership

The Box is not intended to apply to income derived from passive investment in IP. Qualifying patents must be actively owned, which broadly means that the company must be performing a significant amount of management activity in respect of the patent (eg maintaining protection, granting licences, researching alternative applications).

What income falls in the Box?

The mechanism to calculate income that is subject to the 10% Patent Box rate is complex but broadly, and subject to certain adjustments, worldwide income from the following activities falls within the Box:

☐ sales of patented items or items incorporating patented items;

☐ licence fees and royalties from patented items;

☐ sales of patents;

☐ any infringement actions;

☐ deemed royalties for the internal use of a patent in activities that do not directly generate patent income (eg the use of a patent in the provision of services).

The Patent Box therefore has wide potential application - it is only necessary for one component of an item to be patented for the income derived from sales of the entire item to fall within the Box.

Changes to the regime

The UK and Germany agreed at the end of 2014 to change the UK Patent Box tax incentive scheme.

This is not the end of the Patent Box - under the current proposals the Patent Box regime will in fact remain in place until at least June 2021 for current beneficiaries.

From June 2016 it is expected that a new beneficial tax incentive agreed on by all EU member states will be implemented, so UK businesses should continue to be able to benefit from patent-related tax relief.

The scheme has attracted opposition from a number of EU member states, in particular from Germany, on the basis that it could potentially provide an incentive for profits to be shifted artificially to the UK from other countries in order to benefit from the reduced tax rate. This would represent a breach of EU rules on tax competition.

Changes to the UK Patent Box regime have therefore been announced, although more detail is still awaited

CHAPTER 27
WHEN NON RESIDENT COMPANIES ARE WITHIN THE UK CORPORATION TAX REGIME

Foreign businesses should be able to undertake significant UK activity without triggering tax liabilities.

Corporation Tax

The UK levies corporation tax on the world-wide income and chargeable gains of companies that are resident. As recently as 2008 the mainstream corporation tax rate was 30% but, in line with its policy of increasing the competitiveness of the UK, the coalition government has reduced the mainstream rate every year since coming to power. From April 2015 the corporation tax will be 20% for most UK companies.

A company incorporated in the UK will almost inevitably be tax resident there, but a foreign company which is "centrally managed and controlled" from the UK is also taxed as a UK resident.

The management and control test looks at the highest level of strategic control over a company's affairs. In the majority of cases this will be exercised by the Board of Directors in its formal meetings called to decide company policy. If those meetings take place in the UK the company will be UK resident, subject to the "tie-breaker article" under an applicable double tax treaty.

The location of a company's central management and control is a question of fact, and it may not always be exercised at Board meetings.

For example, occasionally the usual functions of a Board may be carried out by some other committee or person such as a dominant director or a corporate managing agent, or the Board members may exercise their powers outside the formal Board meetings.

HMRC has explained its approach to this issue as follows:

* it first tries to ascertain whether the Board in fact exercises central management and control or whether it is exercised by some other person(s);

* if power does rest with the Board, HMRC seeks to determine where the directors exercise this central management and control (which is not necessarily where they meet); and

* in cases where the directors apparently do not exercise central management and control of the company, HMRC then looks to establish where and by whom it is exercised.

Biggest risk of being controlled from the UK?

Although any company incorporated outside the UK is subject to a theoretical risk of becoming UK tax resident under the central management and control test, that risk is greatest in relation to structured intermediaries which have a limited purpose within a corporate group or financing structure, so-called "special purpose vehicles" or "SPVs".

SPVs are commonly established in low, or no, tax jurisdictions with the intention, usually, to achieve tax neutrality and avoid "tax leakage" rather than to realise a positive tax advantage.

Although an SPV may undertake numerous transactions, perhaps regularly receiving and distributing payment streams, substantially all such transactions will be prescribed at the inception of the transaction or effected by a contractual counter-party under some form of asset management agreement.

A defining characteristic of such SPVs is that they do not usually initiate new transactions on their own account and the ongoing involvement of the Board is potentially minimal which increases the risk that some other person may be viewed as controlling the company.

Where there is a risk, whether because of the composition of the Board, the delegation of management responsibilities or some other factor, that control of an offshore entity may be exercised from the UK it is advisable to seek legal advice on the appropriate control and record keeping procedures necessary to create, and
evidence, a factual defence against an HMRC challenge.

Permanent Establishment

For the majority of non-UK companies that begin to develop a UK customer-base the most significant "tipping point" will concern the level of UK activity which is possible without going so far as to establish a taxable presence.

A non-UK company that maintains its control offshore may nevertheless become subject to UK corporation tax if it begins to carry on any part of its trade through a UK "permanent establishment".

In that case, subject to the terms of an applicable double tax treaty, tax will be charged on its UK profits or, more likely, the profits it would have earned from its UK activity had all it business been undertaken on an arm's length basis in compliance with the UK's transfer pricing rules.

A "permanent establishment" usually means a branch office or other fixed place of business, in which case there is seldom much doubt as to whether one has been established. However, a taxable presence may also be established simply by engaging one or more dependent agents who have the authority to conclude contracts on
behalf of the foreign company and who regularly do so with customers in the UK.

At first sight this might suggest that a company will be liable for corporation tax immediately if it puts employees or representatives "on the ground" in the UK. But, not every form of business activity performed in the UK, whether through a branch or a dependent agent, will trigger corporation tax liabilities.

A company that may be considering engaging UK based personnel for the first time or even establishing a UK office on a speculative basis may be able to arrange its preliminary steps so as to delay the point at which tax registration, reporting and payment obligations may arise.

Whilst a company is merely testing the UK demand for its products or services it may be possible to restrict the activity of its UK personnel so as to avoid crossing the trading threshold. So, for example, if the role of the agents is limited to marketing, so that any contracts being entered into are either on standard terms or executed outside the UK by the company rather than on its behalf
by the UK agent, it should be possible to avoid trading at least until it becomes clear that there is a viable market for the company in the UK.

Similarly, if the activities of the branch are limited to publicity, research and customer support, making it, in effect, a "representative office", actual trading and, consequently, UK corporation tax may be avoided.

Careful structuring to avoid having a permanent establishment can lead to significant tax savings. For instance its been stated that despite having UK sales in excess of £3.3 billion Amazon pays no UK corporation tax because it carries on only an "order fulfillment" business in the UK with a Luxembourg entity being the legal supplier of goods.

CHAPTER 28
TRADING IN THE UK WITH A UK COMPANY OR LLP

If you're a non UK resident looking to carry out any business activities in the UK you should carefully consider whether there could be a charge to UK tax, and if so how this can be mitigated.

As we've seen in the previous chapter as a non UK resident you are generally outside the scope of UK tax provided you aren't engaged in a UK trade via a UK permanent establishment.

One of the two circumstances in which there can be a permanent establishment is where there is a fixed place of business in the UK through which the trade is carried on.

Agency

The other occasion when there can be a permanent establishment is where there is a UK dependent agent.

The tax legislation treats the following as a permanent establishment:

'…an agent acting on behalf of the company where the agent has and habitually exercises here authority to do business on behalf of the company. As long as that agent is not of independent status acting in the ordinary course of his business."

So if you have someone in the UK acting on your behalf and being able to enter into contracts on your behalf (ie binding you as the offshore principal) they would themselves represent a permanent establishment and lead the way for you to be taxed on the UK profits.

You'd therefore need to ensure that you had no UK agent.

Using an offshore company

The best option if you're non resident may be to use a non UK resident company. This would completely avoid UK corporation tax and also reduce any UK disclosure.

You could consider a company in the Isle of Man which offers 0% corporation tax and can also obtain an EU VAT number.

If you're non resident there would be no issues in terms of the company being UK resident and if there is no UK permanent establishment there would be no UK corporation tax on the profits.

In addition if the receipts are not royalties they wouldn't be subject to UK withholding tax. Receipts could be payable into either a UK or IOM bank account and based on the assumptions above there should be no UK tax due.

Double tax treaties would not be an issue with an offshore company as there is unlikely to be a treaty in place. Note that there is a limited treaty between the UK and IOM which effectively provides that profits in the UK would be taxable to the extent there is a permanent establishment.

This is therefore similar to the UK's s domestic provisions. If using an offshore company was not an option and you wanted to use a UK entity, you could use either a UK company or a UK limited liability partnership.

UK company

If using a UK company, it would be charged to UK corporation tax on its worldwide income and gains. The most effective option would be to use the UK company as an agency company contracting with the clients but not being classed as an agent for the definition of the permanent establishment provisions (eg no power to bind the offshore principal/independent agent and no UK fixed place of business).

The receipts would be taken via the UK company, and paid to you or another offshore entity less a small commission (eg 5%). The commission rate would need to be set at a market rate and the income of the company would be the 5% received.

It could then offset any expenses etc before corporation tax was applied.

The UK company would not be taxed on the entire income it received on behalf of an offshore principal but it would clearly be taxed on it's commission receipts.

The downsides to this are that UK accounts and an annual return would need to be filed along with corporation tax returns. Shareholders and Directors details would need to be disclosed to the UK tax authorities.

UK reporting

In terms of the accounts for the UK company it would be essential to determine whether for accounting purposes it acted as principal or agent.

UK reporting standards state that in order for a company to be viewed as a principal it should normally have exposure to all significant benefits and risks associated with at least one of the following:

(a) Selling price: the ability, within economic constraints, to establish the selling price with the customer, either directly or, where the selling price of an item is fixed,indirectly by providing additional goods or services or adjusting the terms of a linked transaction; or

(b) Stock: exposure to the risks of damage, slow movement and obsolescence, and changes in suppliers' prices.

Where the seller has not disclosed that it is acting as agent, there is a rebuttable presumption that it is acting as principal.

Additional factors which indicate that a seller may be acting as principal include:

(a) performance of part of the services, or modification to the goods supplied;

(b) assumption of credit risk; and

(c) discretion in supplier selection.

By contrast where a seller acts as agent it will not normally be exposed to the majority of the benefits and risks associated with the transaction. Agency arrangements will typically include the following characteristics:

(a) the seller has disclosed the fact that it is acting as agent;

(b) once the seller has confirmed its customer's order with a third party, the seller will normally have no further involvement in the performance of the ultimate supplier's contractual obligations;

(c) the amount that the seller earns is predetermined, being either a fixed fee per transaction or a stated percentage of the amount billed to the customer; and

(d) the seller bears no stock or credit risk, other than in circumstances where it receives additional consideration from the ultimate supplier in return for its assumption of this risk.

Where the substance of a transaction is that the company acts as agent, it should report as turnover in the accounts the commission received in return for its performance under the agency arrangement.

Any amounts received that are payable to the offshore principal would not be included in the agent's turnover.

You'd therefore need to determine whether the UK company could be classed as an agent for the purposes of the accounts. As stated above it looks at the substance of the transaction and there is a rebuttable presumption that if there's no disclosure of the principal that the UK company would be the principal (and therefore report all the turnover and the subsequent payments back to the offshore company).

Limited Liability Partnership ('LLP')

The alternative option would be to use an LLP. This is a pass through entity for UK tax purposes and therefore the income would be attributed to you personally. Providing the profits are not profits of a UK trade and you are non UK resident there would be no UK income tax charge on the profits.

This therefore has an advantage over the UK Ltd company above in that it can avoid all UK tax.

In terms of disclosure the notes to the Partnership return specifically state that '…Where all the partners are not resident in the UK, the Partnership Tax Return should enter only the profits arising from UK operations…'.

Therefore if the partnership had no UK trading profit the partnership return would effectively be blank.

The downside of an LLP is that it would need to file accounts with companies house showing it's profit and loss account and balance sheet, even though it may conduct it's business entirely overseas.

CHAPTER 29
WATCH OUT FOR THE NEW ANTI AVOIDANCE RULE ON THE TRANSFER OF CORPORATE PROFITS

The Government has introduced a new anti-avoidance measure, targeted at businesses operating through a group structure where there is, in substance, a significant "payment" of profits from one company to another.

Set out below is a summary of how the new rule works, and how it might apply to certain, what might up to now have been seen as commercial, arrangements.

A new section 1305A will be inserted into the Corporation Tax Act 2009 and will apply where:

- two companies (A and B) are part of the same "group"; and

- A and B are party to "arrangements"; which

- result, in substance, in A (directly or indirectly) making a payment to B of "all or a significant part" of A's profits (or the profits of another group company); and

- one of the main purposes of the arrangements is to secure a "tax advantage" (and not necessarily for A or B).

Section 1305A, as currently drafted, is capable of wide application because "group", "arrangements" and "tax advantage" are each also given a wide meaning. Although the securing of a tax advantage (which includes a "reduction" in tax paid or payable) must be a main purpose of the arrangements, in the current climate this may not be a high hurdle for HMRC to overcome.

Although it might be thought that the requirement for a "payment" of profit from A to B might limit the ambit of section 1305A:

- the section is headed "Avoidance schemes involving the transfer [our emphasis] of corporate profits"; and

- the arrangements which are caught are those that "result in what is, in substance, a payment (directly or indirectly) from A to B of ... a significant part [not defined] of A's profits". In our view this may equate a transfer with a payment.

If section 1305A applies, A's profits for corporation tax purposes must be recalculated as though the arrangements leading to the profit transfer had not occurred.

Unlike some anti-avoidance provisions, section 1305A does not contain a "commercial" let out. If the arrangements produce a transfer of profits, which in turn causes a reduction in tax take, the arrangements may be ignored for tax purposes.

HMRC guidance

In practice, draft guidance on the operation of section 1305A, recently published by HMRC, indicates that they will not normally challenge arrangements if:

- they are ordinary commercial arrangements; and

- they are also arrangements of a kind that are usually entered into by companies operating in the same type of business.

For example, HMRC states that intra-group reinsurance, affected as part of "ordinary commercial arrangements", would "not normally" fall within the scope of section 1305A. An example given by HMRC of "ordinary commercial" reinsurance is where the profitability of the ceding company is taken into account in determining the premium payable.

What have, up to now, been seen as commercial arrangements that might be under threat include:

- the aggressive use of reinsurance;
- the use of offshore (normally tax haven or low tax jurisdiction) group companies;
- aggressive finance and group treasury arrangements;
- the placing of profitable business in low tax or tax exempt group companies
- profit related royalties and transfer payments.

It is possible that HMRC may be tempted to use section 1305A to attack the tax arrangements, recently much publicised, entered into by certain US multi-national retailers with a substantial UK presence.

The guidance gives the example of an online retailer which concludes contracts with UK customers through a non-UK resident company. The conclusion on such an arrangement leaves many questions unanswered -- unhelpfully HMRC merely confirm that such arrangement will be caught by section 1305A if it involves a "transfer of profits".

CHAPTER 30
LIQUIDATING COMPANIES IN 2015

The tax treatment of company distributions on a winding up have changed significantly from 1 March 2012. In this chapter we look at how the new rules operate and any tax planning opportunities available.

Old Rules

Under the "old rules" (ESC C16) it was possible for a distribution made on the winding-up of a company to be taxed as a capital receipt in the hands of the shareholder.

In many cases capital treatment is preferred to income treatment as it means that CGT is payable at 28% (if a higher rate taxpayer) or 10% (if Entrepreneurs Relief is available).

If it wasn't classed as a capital distribution it would be taxed as a dividend at either 25% or 36.11% if the shareholders income was above the basic rate band.

New rules

New legislation has been introduced which states that a distribution made on or after 1 March 2012 will be taxed as a capital receipt where the following conditions are satisfied:

☐ the distribution must have been made by the company in anticipation of the company's winding up

☐ the company must have secured, or must have intended to secure, the payment of any sums due to it;

☐ the company must have satisfied, or must have intended to satisfy, any debts or liabilities; and

☐ the amount of the distribution (or the total of that distribution and any earlier "relevant" distributions) must not exceed the cap of £25,000.

Capital treatment will be withdrawn if the company has not been dissolved and has either:

(1) failed to satisfy all of its debts and liabilities; or

(2) failed to secure all payments due to it, within two years.

So the big change is that capital treatment will only apply on the winding up (as opposed to a full liquidation) if the extraction is less than £25,000.

Applying the cap

Now that we have a cap, we must apply it and there are three important points to note here:

(1) the cap applies by reference to the distributions made by the company and not to the distributions received by a shareholder (although it is the shareholder that will feel the effect of the legislation).

The cap will be breached if the total relevant distributions made by the company exceed £25,000. This is the case regardless of whether or not the amount received by the recipient exceeds £25,000;

(2) any earlier relevant distributions must be taken into account in determining if a relevant distribution breaches the cap. Remember that any distributions made when the company 'intends' to wind up are relevant distributions.

(3)the cap applies on an all or nothing basis. If a relevant distribution exceeds £25,000 then all of that distribution will be taxed as income in the hands of the shareholder, not just the excess amount.

There are a number of potential problems here not least how to determine if a distribution is a relevant distribution. At what point does a company intend to wind up?

There will also be compliance issues in some cases such as where a dividend is received by a minority shareholder in a company in which he or she has had little involvement. Will that shareholder be in a position to know the total amount of relevant distributions made by the company?

Planning points

Here's some of the key planning points:

☐ Firstly capital treatment may not necessarily be preferred. Where the amount of the distribution is only within the shareholders basic rate band, an income distribution would be preferred anyway (as this would be tax free).

☐ The cap only applies to distributions on a winding up. You can still secure capital treatment for larger distributions if you opt for a full liquidation. Of course the downside will be the increased cost, but where larger amounts are extracted the income tax savings could easily cover this.

☐ There are other opportunities to extract capital distributions. Most notably where the company has a large share capital and you reduce that share capital. This would be paid to the shareholder and taxed as a capital distribution. The £25,000 cap would not apply to this and therefore capital treatment for amounts larger than £25,000 could be obtained.

☐ Although the cap is "all or nothing", if the amount to be extracted is larger than this it could be attractive to pay an income distribution while the company is still trading, and then extract the remaining cash (less than £25,000) when the company is being wound up. Remember that the income dividend would need to be paid before the company had an intention to be wound up.

CHAPTER 31
TRANSFERRING PROPERTY ASSETS OUT OF A

COMPANY TAX EFFICIENTLY

A common scenario is for a company to hold both trading and investment assets. This could be because the shareholders have decided to use retained cash in the company to purchase investment properties or other investment assets (in the belief that this saves on the tax charge on extracting funds from the company).

Alternatively it may simply be the case that assets that were previously used for trading purposes (eg property) are now held as an investment.

This is usually fine until you start to think about the future disposal of either the property or the trade.

Taking a disposal of the trade, there would usually be no problem with this and the shareholders could consider a sale of the shares in the company. This can be very tax efficient and Entrepreneurs Relief will often reduce the tax rate to 10% providing the investment assets aren't "substantial" in relation to the other trading activities/assets. If there are substantial non trading assets the rate of CGT can increase to 28%.

It is usually therefore advised to separate the investment from the trading activities. How you actually do this without paying a fortune in tax though is another question.

A simple transfer of the property from the company to the shareholders or another company would be a disposal by the original company. As such a gain would arise based on the market value of the property (usually). If the shareholders are UK resident the transfer at undervalue would also be taxed on them as though they had received a dividend. This would then be subject to income tax on the element of undervalue.

So all in all this is not really a good option.

Another option which may be preferable could be to consider a demerging of the existing company, with the separation of the trading and the investment activities. There are specific tax provisions that provide for CGT reliefs on a demerger applicable to trading companies or the insolvency act could be used. The existing trading company could probably be liquidated during this process, and the assets split into newco's.

Under this the existing company is placed in liquidation and in essence the liquidator transfers the assets to newcos established by the shareholders, in exchange for the issue of shares to the shareholders(eg X Ltd & Y Ltd).

They could then dispose of the shares in X Ltd directly without the need to crystalize a gain on Y Ltd. This treatment can also apply for investment assets and the shares in X and Y Ltd would be treated as being owned for the same holding period as the existing trading company.

Therefore Newco X could receive the Investment property and Newco Y could receive the trading assets. The newcos would remain owned by the existing shareholders and they could then sell the trading company separately from the investment asset/company. Note that these are all complex areas and should be looked at in some significant detail.

In terms of stamp duty if the shareholding proportions will be the same as they were for the current company (ie the owners would have exactly the same percentage shareholdings in X Ltd as they currently have in the trading company) it should be possible to avoid stamp duty on this transfer, although the anti avoidance provisions would need to be reviewed in detail.

The shareholders could then dispose of the shares in X Ltd or Y Ltd. A gain would arise with Entrepreneurs Relief potentially applying. This would still represent a significant tax saving in many cases when compared with a company disposal of assets (although clearly the specific facts would need to be considered eg the base cost of shares/assets, any capital losses etc).

Therefore if you're looking at splitting an existing trading company a demerger could be considered. Note that ideally this should be done a significant period before a disposal of the shares to a third party purchaser, although if necessary the liquidation route may be considered for disposals shortly after the reorganisation.

32 CHANGES TO DIVIDENDS IN THE 2015 SUMMER BUDGET

Significant changes to the tax treatment of dividends were announced in the 2015 Summer Budget.

The dividend tax credit which is currently a 1/9 notional tax credit and is offset against income tax will be replaced by a new £5,000 tax-free dividend allowance for all taxpayers from April 2016. Tax rates on dividend income will be increased as well.

The Chancellor stated that 85% of those with dividends will not pay more, or will have their tax cut. However this applies to portfolio investors. For anyone that's using a company to carry out their trade or investment this will have a dramatic effect on their tax liability.

From April 2016 the government will remove the Dividend Tax Credit and replace it with a new tax-free Dividend Allowance of £5,000 a year for all taxpayers.

This means that a standard taxpayer will have:

Personal allowance = £11,000

Dividend allowance = £5,000

Total tax free allowance = £16,000

Under the new system, everyone who receives dividend income won't pay tax on the first £5,000. Basic rate taxpayers will pay 7.5% tax on any additional dividend income, higher rate taxpayers will pay 32.5% and additional rate taxpayers 38.1%.

HMRC state:

"...While these rates remain below the main rates of income tax, those who receive significant dividend income -- for example due to very large shareholdings (typically more than £140,000) or as a result of receiving significant dividends through a closed company -- will pay more. These changes will also start to reduce the incentive to incorporate and remunerate through dividends rather than through wages to reduce tax liabilities..."

Therefore it's pretty clear that they are looking to reduce the tax benefits of using a company to trade, particularly where a dividend extraction is used.

Example 1

Jack has a trading company Jack Ltd that has profits of £100,000.

Current rules

Under the current rules the company would pay corporation tax of £20,000. If he was a higher rate taxpayer and extracted the remaining £80,000 he'd pay tax of

Net dividend = £80,000
Tax credit (1/9) = £8,888
Gross dividend = £88,888
Income tax at 32.5% = £28,888
Less tax credit = -£8,888
Income tax payable = £20,000

New rules

Under the new rules he'd be taxed differently on the £80,000 dividends. Assuming he is still a higher rate taxpayer he wouldn't have his personal allowance to offset and would just offset his £5,000 dividend allowance.

His taxable dividends would therefore be £75,000. He'd then be taxed at 32.5% on these leading to an income tax liability of £24,375. This is an increase of £4,375 in income tax.

Example 2

Steve provides garden services through a limited company. For 2016--17, he takes a salary equal to the personal allowance and receives dividends of £45,000. The basic rate band is £31,900.

Simon will pay tax on his dividends as follows:

£5,000 Dividend allowance @ 0% = 0

Dividends within the Basic Rate Band = £26,900* @ 7.5% = £2,027

Dividends within the Higher Rate Band = £13,100 @ 32.5% = £4,258

Total tax = £6,285

(*£31,900 less £5,000)

The impact on company incorporations

It is common for a person trading through a limited company to take a small salary and any additional funds as dividends. In most situations, this gives the best tax result as it avoids or reduces exposure to NICs. It also gives a good tax result compared to trading on a self-employed basis, again because of the NICs saving.

This is illustrated by the following table (Table 1) which shows the tax liability for each business vehicle at various profit limits based on 2015/16 rates, etc. and assuming that the company pays a salary of £8,060 and that all remaining profits are taken as dividends.

Current Tax			
Profits	Tax Sole Trader	Tax Company	Saving
£20,000	3,100	2,388	712

£30,000	6,000	4,388	1,612
£40,000	8,900	6,388	2,512
£50,000	12,790	9,053	3,737

However, these savings will reduce significantly from April 2016 when the new rules for taxing dividends take effect. This is illustrated by Table 2. Note that in this table, the tax liabilities have been calculated using the rates, etc. applying for 2015/16 but taking into account the new rules for taxing dividends as set out above.

Tax From 2016			
Profits	Tax Sole Trader	Tax Company	Saving
£20,000	3,100	2,539	561
£30,000	6,000	5,139	861
£40,000	8,900	7,739	1,161
£50,000	12,790	10,339	2,451

As can be seen from the table above, there are still tax savings to be had. And remember that in arriving at the figures above, I have assumed that the trader will want to withdraw all of the profits. If some of the profits can be retained in the company then the immediate tax liability will be reduced.

Is salary now more attractive than dividends following the Summer Budget?

Actually when you do the figures it becomes clear that (if you ignore the £5,000 exemption) everybody is going to pay an extra 7.5% tax on their dividends -- whatever their tax bands.
0% goes up to 7.5%; 25% goes up to 32.5% and 30.6% goes up to 38.1%.

This is certainly going to give rise to some changes. Nobody is likely to pay 20% corporation tax and then 38% on a dividend.

The decisions about whether to incorporate will therefore be seriously affected and so will the interaction between salaries and dividends.

There are lots of permutations but the issue is really about how the individual can get the maximum amount in his hands with the minimum tax liability. In this equation a salary will nearly always be better than a dividend because the corporation tax relief will always outweigh the additional NIC cost.

OTHER BOOKS FROM THE AUTHOR

Tax Planning With Double Tax Treaties 2015+

This guide contains detailed information on how you can use the terms of the UK's double tax treaties to reduce your UK tax liability. It is updated for the latest anti avoidance rules that apply from . . . keep reading

Tax Planning With Holding Companies: 2015+

Structures such as the "Double Irish" and the "Dutch Sandwich" have gained press attention due to being used by various multinational groups to reduce their effective tax rate. Al . . . keep reading

Offshore Companies Holding UK Property: 2015+

In this book we look in detail at precisely how offshore companies owning UK property are taxed, taking account of the tax changes in 2013 and 2014 as well as the planned changes in 2015 and 2016. . . . keep reading

How To Avoid CGT In 2014/2015

This book looks in detail at how you can reduce capital gains tax in 2014/2015. The CGT reliefs are one of the main ways that most people reduce CGT. We therefore look at all of the main reliefs in d . . . keep reading

Royalty Tax Planning 2014: Strategies & Tactics To Reduce Tax

Royalties present particular and unique challenges when it comes to tax planning. Not only do many companies own intellectual property,

writing and selling both printed books and e-books online is b . . . keep
reading

Family Tax Planning Handbook 2014: Strategies & Tactics To Reduce Tax
n many ways one of the simplest ways to reduce tax is to hold assets
and split income with your spouse and children/grandchildren.
However, whilst there are numerous tax benefits available there ar . . .
keep reading

Tax Planning For Termination Payments

If you're receiving a severance package, ensuring that you qualify for all
your available tax exemptions/reliefs is important. In this book we
summarise how these will app . . . keep reading

UK Agency/Nominee Structure 2014

Using a UK company as an agent for an offshore Principal can be
attractive for both tax and asset protection purposes. In this book we
summarise how this will operate and h . . . keep reading

Offshore Structuring 2014

In this book we look at some of the key offshore tax planning concepts
and opportunities for 2014. . . . keep reading

Offshore Companies: 15 Ways To Reduce Taxes

There are a number of complex anti avoidance rules that can apply
where offshore, non-resident companies are used for UK tax planning.
In this book we look at 15 of the ma . . . keep reading

Tax Planning For Entrepreneurs Relief 2014/2015

There are a number of hoops to jump through in order to claim
Entrepreneurs relief and reduce your rate of CGT to 10%. In particular

you need to ensure that the assets sold are "qualifying assets . . . keep reading

Inheritance Tax Planning Handbook 2014/2015: Strategies & Tactics To Save Inheritance Tax

Inheritance tax is a particularly nasty tax as it's a tax on your capital that you've accumulated from your after tax earnings. In this book we look at some of the top ways you can legally reduce your . . . keep reading

Tax Planning With Trusts 2014

Trusts offer a highly attractive way to pass wealth onto other family members in a tax efficient manner. In this book we look at when and how both UK and offshore trusts can be used to reduce UK inco . . . keep reading

E-Commerce Tax Planning 2014/2015

If you're trading via a website or are involved in other e-commerce activities there are a number of tax planning opportunities available. In this book we look at tax planning for all types of e-comm . . . keep reading

CGT Planning For UK Property: 2015 & Beyond

Over recent years there have been changes to the capital gains tax (CGT) treatment of UK residential property held by companies. Further changes are to be made from 2015 and 2016 which will have a mas . . . keep reading

Tax Planning For The Statutory Residence Test: 2014/2015

The new Statutory Residence Test ("SRT") applies from April 2013 and aims to provide a comprehensive method of clearly establishing when an individual will (and won't) be UK resident. In thi . . . keep reading

Tax Planning For Property Developers: 2014/2015

If you are trading or are planning to trade or develop property, a key consideration will be reducing the amount of UK tax charged on the profits from the development. In this guide we look at how p . . . keep reading

Buy To Let Tax Planning In 2014/2015

Buy To Let ("BTL") landlords have to consider Income tax, Capital gains tax, Inheritance tax and Stamp duty land tax on their property holdings. In this book we look at tax planning techni . . . keep reading

Working Overseas: The Complete Tax Planning Guide 2014/2015

If you're working overseas either as a permanent move or under a short term secondment you should carefully consider the tax planning opportunities available to you. Many people look to go and work ov . . . keep reading

Non-Resident and Offshore Tax Planning 2014/2015: How To Cut Your Tax To Zero

This brand new (March 2014) edition of our best selling offshore tax planning book tells you what you need to know to take advantage of offshore opportunities and slash your UK tax bill. It's a pretty . . . keep reading

The World's Best Tax Havens 2014/2015

This book provides a rare insight into the glamorous world of tax havens and is fully updated for the latest 2014/2015 changes. The first half contains fascinating information on 25 of the world's b . . . keep reading

How To Avoid Tax On Overseas Property 2014/2015

Of increasing importance to property investors are overseas property developments. Investors looking to benefit from higher levels of capital growth often look overseas. This opens up even more tax pl . . . keep reading

Tax Planning For The Family Home

For many people the family home is the most valuable asset they have. As such protecting its value will be key importance. In this tax guide we look at the key tax planning opportunities for the fam . . . keep reading

Offshore Tax Secrets 2014

Although there are now a raft of anti avoidance rules that apply to all sorts of offshore planning, for the well advised there are still opportunities available. In this guide we look at some of the to . . . keep reading

Inheritance Tax Planning For Non UK Domiciliaries

Non UK domiciliaries are in a privileged position when it comes to UK Inheritance tax planning. So long as they can retain their non UK domicile status they can avoid UK inheritance tax on their overs . . . keep reading

Tax Planning With LLP's

In this guide we look at exactly how an LLP is taxed, before looking at how you can use LLP's to reduce your UK taxes. We cover how LLP's can be used by individuals as well as companies for UK tax pla . . . keep reading

Offshore Tax Planning For UK Companies In 2014

If you're interested in offshore tax planning involving UK companies there are plenty of opportunities available.I n this guide we show you how and when you can . . . keep reading

Offshore Telecommuting: How To Avoid Taxes and Live and Work Offshore

Telecommuting is one of the hot topics at the moment. You've probably read of people sitting on a beach in the Caribbean working from their laptop, or sitting on board their boat moored in Cyprus and . . . keep reading

Tax Planning For Fiscal Nomads & Perpetual Travellers

Many people enjoy going on their summer holidays as a tourist in a foreign country. How would you fancy extending this 'holiday' permanently? The basic principle is to exploit the residency rules in a . . . keep reading

Where To Base Your Offshore Company

There are a lot of firms offering to create low cost offshore companies, but which jurisdiction should you choose? In this mini guide we look at how offshore companies can be used and some of the top . . . keep reading

Selling Your Business 2013

If you're selling your business or company this is an essential read. The tax at stake could be significant and this 170 page book goes through in detail the tax planning opportunities available to yo . . . keep reading

How To Legally Pay Less Tax: 34 Top Tips

By undertaking simple tax planning many people can significantly reduce the amount of tax they pay. In this guide we look at 34 top tax tips to reduce income tax, capital gains tax, inheritance tax an . . . keep reading

Tax Planning For Property Investors 2013/2014

Many people own properties that are let out and held as investments. These properties can generate an income and hopefully a capital gain on the eventual disposal. This 110 page guide looks at tax p . . . keep reading

Tax Planning For Dividends

With the highest income tax rate now 45%, and a maximum effective tax rate on dividends of 30.55%, any planning opportunities to reduce this can be very attractive. In this guide we look at precisel . . . keep reading

Tax Planning With Excluded Property Trusts

In this book we look in detail at precisely how Excluded Property Trusts can be used to reduce UK Inheritance tax, Income tax and Capital gains tax. This book is updated for the latest 2013 changes an . . . keep reading

ABOUT THE AUTHOR

Lee Hadnum LLB ACA CTA is an international tax specialist. He is a Chartered Accountant and Chartered Tax Adviser and is the Editor of the popular tax planning website:

 www.wealthprotectionreport.co.uk

Lee is also the author of a number of best selling tax planning books.

Other Tax Guides

- **Tax Planning Techniques Of The Rich & Famous** - Essential reading for anyone who wants to use the same tax planning techniques as the most successful Entrepreneurs, large corporations and celebrities

- **The Worlds Best Tax Havens 2014/2015** – 220 page book looking at the worlds best offshore jurisdictions in detail

- **Non Resident & Offshore Tax Planning 2014/2015 –** Offshore tax planning for UK residents or anyone looking to purchase UK property or trade in the UK. A comprehensive guide.

- **Tax Planning With Offshore Companies & Trusts: The A-Z Guide** - Detailed analysis of when and how you can use offshore companies and trusts to reduce your UK taxes

- **Tax Planning For Company Owners 2014/2015** – How company owners can reduce income tax, corporation tax and NICs

- **How To Avoid CGT In 2013/2014** – Tax planning for anyone looking to reduce UK capital gains tax

- **Buy To Let Tax Planning 2014/2015** – How property investors can reduce income tax, CGT and inheritance tax

- **Asset Protection Handbook** – Looks at strategies to ringfence your assets in today's increasing litigious climate

- **Working Overseas Guide** – Comprehensive analysis of how you can save tax when working overseas

- **Double Tax Treaty Planning** – How you can use double tax treaties to reduce UK taxes

Printed in Great Britain
by Amazon.co.uk, Ltd.,
Marston Gate.